EVERYONE
CAN DO
SOMETHING

EVERYONE CAN DO SOMETHING

A FIELD GUIDE FOR STRATEGICALLY RALLYING YOUR CHURCH AROUND THE ORPHANED AND VULNERABLE

JASON JOHNSON

**NATIONAL DIRECTOR OF CHURCH MINISTRY INITIATIVES,
CHRISTIAN ALLIANCE FOR ORPHANS**

CAFO | CHURCH *ministry*

credo
house publishers

INTRODUCTION

Many churches around the country are taking bold, noble and exciting steps towards responding to God's call to care for orphans and vulnerable children in unprecedented ways. It's a historic time in the Church, one which generations to come will undoubtedly recognize as a time when God moved mightily through His people to press into a matter that is near to His heart. It's an exciting time, yet it's also a time filled with many questions regarding what to do with an orphan and vulnerable children's ministry. Many are passionate, ready and eager to establish thoughtful strategies, sustainable systems and realistic next steps for their people. The question is not should they do it; it's how should they do it.

The goal of this book is to answer that question in a way that is theologically rooted and practically implementable in a variety of different types of churches. Whether it's a church of 100 or a church of 10,000, one campus or dozens around the city, a rural country church or an urban core city church, a new church plant or a historic downtown church, the question of how to start and lead an orphan care ministry is prevalent and some key principles are universal no matter the context, structure, rhythm or culture of the church.

This book is intended for two groups of people:

• Those just beginning to take steps towards establishing an orphan and vulnerable children's ministry in their church.

• Those seeking to incorporate principles of movement, growth and sustainability in their ministry towards orphans and vulnerable children which already exists.

Everyone Can Do Something is written for the pastor, the church staff member or the faithful and passionate volunteer that is taking the lead on this ministry in their church. It is not a prescriptive manual that speaks to every unique situation and circumstance at every church — no one book can do that. Instead, it is an outline of principles to explore, strategies to consider and practices to implement in an adaptable, contextual way that fits best within the uniqueness of your own church.

This book is most effectively read within the context of community — an existing ministry leadership team or a few passionate people that want to see one formed. An understanding of the culture of your church and an awareness of the values, rhythms and processes it operates by will be invaluable as you explore the concepts in this book and consider how they may be most effectively implemented into your unique culture. Some parts of this book will be directly applicable to your ministry today and some will not be. You will have to discern what you are capable of doing now or in the near future and what might need to be held off as a part of your more long-term ministry strategy.

Finally, know this — wherever you are on this journey and whatever it is you are currently facing in your ministry — your work is worth it, and you are not alone. You are part of a movement of people that are actively engaging their churches with the message that "everyone can do something" to care for vulnerable children and families in a variety of unique and creative ways.

Press on! It's worth it.

Now, let's get started.

CHAPTERS

1

BUILDING HEALTHY LEADERSHIP

The importance of building a leadership team early on in the ministry cannot be overstated. No one person, or couple, can carry the weight of the ministry long-term alone. A team is required, however formal or informal you choose to set it up. Among other things, the benefits of building a team include:

- Tasks are spread out over a few, not isolated to one or two individuals to carry the whole. (responsibility)

- Growth is not dependent upon the capacity of one, but on the collective energy of a team. (scalability)

- The ministry's long-term impact is shared, not dependent upon the stamina of one. (sustainability)

- A healthy environment of support encourages creativity, passion and commitment. (community)

- The unique gifts, passions and perspectives of a team minimize bias and promotes creativity. (diversity)

- A leadership team communicates "where to go and who to talk to" for others in the church. (clarity)

❷ What other benefits of building a strong leadership team can you identify?

❷ How have you experienced some of these benefits in your current team?

❷ What changes do you need to make to maximize these benefits through your team?

THREE KEY ROLES OF A LEADER

1. MULTIPLIER

In the early days of Jesus' ministry, all activity was centralized to Him — He preached, He healed, He performed miracles, etc. Yet, at a critical point in His ministry (Matthew 10), He began to decentralize the work by empowering His disciples to do those things. In essence, He multiplied Himself through them — thus multiplying the spread of His ministry.

" " *1 Summoning his twelve disciples, he gave them authority over unclean spirits, to drive them out and to heal every disease and sickness...5 Jesus sent out these twelve after giving them instructions: "Don't take the road that leads to the Gentiles, and don't enter any Samaritan town. 6 Instead, go to the lost sheep of the house of Israel. 7 As you go, proclaim: 'The kingdom of heaven has come near.' 8 Heal the sick, raise the dead, cleanse those with leprosy, drive out demons. Freely you received, freely give.*
Matthew 10:1, 5-8

A multiplier doesn't just tell people what to do; they trust people with what needs to be done. They understand that if they keep doing everything, no one else will do anything. For a multiplying leader, it's not simply an issue of delegation; it's a matter of discipleship — creating space for people to a) identify their unique gifts, and b) use them for the good of the whole (2 Corinthians 12; Romans 12).

2. VISIONARY

A visionary sees what does not yet exist, yet communicates it as if it does. They not only believe certain things should happen, they also show people how they can happen. A visionary leader doesn't use team members to fulfill a mission as much as they empower team members to live out their mission most fully.

It's not about them helping you do something, it's about you empowering them to own the vision and act on it. A visionary leader understands that the vision is bigger than them and can only truly, effectively and sustainability be fulfilled through the collaboration of others.

3. CATALYZER

Nitrogen + Hydrogen = Nothing. However, Nitrogen + Hydrogen + <u>Iron</u> = Ammonia. Once Iron is introduced into the N+H equation, a different outcome is achieved. Oddly enough, when tested, Ammonia has no traces of Iron — just Nitrogen and Hydrogen. Iron is nowhere to be found. That's because it is a catalyst — taking two things and fusing them together to produce an outcome they otherwise would not have been able to produce on their own — and then it gets out of the way. It's not a central ingredient in the final product. It's involvement was crucial and effects are still known, but it's continued presence is not essential to the on-going functioning and ultimate success of the group.

That's what a catalyzing leader does.

In their book, *The Starfish and the Spider*, Ori Brafman and Rod Beckstrom illustrate the power of catalytic leaders by comparing two iconic movies.

> *In a way, the difference between traditional leaders and catalysts is like the difference between Julie Andrew's characters in The Sound of Music and Mary Poppins. In The Sound of Music, Maria enters a dysfunctional family, teaches the children a valuable lesson, convinces the fathers to pay attention to his kids, and shows the family how to get along. Likewise, Mary Poppins visits an equally (albeit charmingly) dysfunctional family, gets equally adorable children to behave, urges equally clueless parents to pay attention to their kids, finds equally effective ways for everyone to get along, and sings equally catchy tunes.*
>
> *At the end of The Sound of Music, though, Maria, after falling in love with the children and the father, sticks around. It's obvious that from now on she'll be the one running the show. Mary Poppins, on the other hand, chim-chim-in-eys right out of London. It's not that Mary Poppins has a fear of commitment. From the very beginning, it's clear that she's come to do a job. Her job is complete when the family can thrive on its own. Once she accomplishes her goal, she rides her umbrella into the sunset.*
>
> *In letting go of the leadership role, the catalyst transfers ownership and responsibility to the circle. Without Mary Poppins, the family takes responsibility for itself.*

A catalyzing leader creates environments in which the ideas of others can flourish. They promote collaboration and creativity and empower others to do work beyond what they ever imagined they could have done. Like Jesus with His disciples, a catalyst teaches, models, empowers and then steps back and let's the team go!

A catalyzing leader creates environments in which the ideas of others can flourish.

FAQ'S ABOUT FORMING A NEW LEADERSHIP TEAM

WHO SHOULD BE ON THE TEAM?

You're not looking for experts, but for passionate people that have the ability to harness that energy in strategic ways for the good of others. One of the best things you can do for the ministry is provide clear direction. Build a team that has the ability to do that — not according to their own biases or agenda, but for the good of those in your church God is calling you to serve.

HOW MANY SHOULD BE ON THE TEAM?

There's no magic number, but a general principle is to build slow and small. The effectiveness of your team is not determined by the quantity of voices at the table but by the quality of each voice at the table. Rally those who can be trusted to steward the development of the vision well. At first that might be just a few, and that's okay. You don't need everyone involved, just the right ones involved for the good of everyone.

WHAT SHOULD OUR TEAM DO?

First and foremost, **pray**. Ask God for clarity, unity, direction and empowerment. Then, **dream** big. What are all of your great ideas? What would you love the ministry to do? Now, **plan** small. What are the few things of highest priority? What things can you realistically implement now and what things need to wait? Your goal is sustainability, not speed. You'll eventually be casting vision, building infrastructure and implementing strategy, but for now pray hard, dream big and plan small. We'll talk about those other things later.

QUESTIONS TO CONSIDER WHEN BUILDING AND LEADING A MINISTRY TEAM

❷ It's important that a leadership team is clearly defined. Right now, who is that team for your ministry? Who would you like for it to be?

❷ What goals do you have for the ministry that those listed above can help cast vision for and implement strategy around?

❷ What are three things you believe the team is currently doing well? What are three things you believe the team could improve on?

❷ What will you do differently in the next 3–6 months to improve on those areas that need growth?

HOW DO I APPROACH MY CHURCH LEADERSHIP?

You've got a great vision for a great purpose and want to get the support of your church staff/pastoral leadership. Now what? What's the best way to approach them with this? Consider the following principles and practices:

ESTABLISH PROOF OF CONCEPT

You are not the only person in the church that is passionate about a particular area of ministry. You are also not the only person in the church asking your church leaders to spend time and energy on a particular area of ministry. The more you can demonstrate how much the ministry is already working and functioning, the better. It provides "proof" that the work is already being done effectively and is meeting a crucial need for people in the church.

PRESENT A STRATEGIC PLAN

This ministry is highly emotional, filled with deeply passionate people in the trenches of foster care and adoption on a daily basis. If we're not careful our emotion and passion can cloud our ability to think methodically and strategically. Church leaders are looking for reasonable, actionable plans for how a ministry focus can be best executed in a way that serves the body best. Put the work in to present a plan that harnesses the passion in a strategic, helpful way.

DON'T LOSE SIGHT OF THE LARGER PICTURE

Church's are complex, having many different moving parts being pulled in many different directions. Often times when pastors are "pitched" great ideas it feels like another pull in another direction. Be mindful and respectful of the fact that church leaders are continually weighing in balance a number of different things. When they say, "This is just another thing," perhaps they don't mean it negatively — they're simply asking you to consider the larger picture.

FLIP YOUR ASSUMPTIONS

If you assume your church leaders don't care about this ministry, you place the burden on them to care and the burden on you to convince them to care. However, if you assume that they do care but that they simply don't know how to care, you place the burden on you to help them know how. It's often the case that a wrong assumption going in creates a wrong approach. Start by flipping the script on your assumptions and see what happens. You might be surprised.

HOW TO HANDLE A CHURCH LEADER THAT DOESN'T "GET IT"

This sentiment is a common one: "We really want this to be a part of our church, but our pastor just doesn't get it." Is that your current reality? One thing to know is that you are not alone. Another is that there's hope. Before you bail to another church, try to aggressively force the issue or just lose hope and give up, here's five alternative ways to respond to the "my pastor doesn't get it" problem.

BE PRAYERFUL
Your responsibility is to pray for a movement, not push an agenda. Pray for the heart of your pastor, that God would stir it in new ways towards the plight of kids in crisis.

BE FAITHFUL
Demonstrate the necessity of an orphan care ministry to your pastor and your church through your actions, not just your words. Continue to be obedient to the call God has placed on your heart and be faithful to fulfill that. In other words, lead by example.

BE HUMBLE
Don't try to implement something good in your church by pointing out all that is bad in it. Communicate with your words and actions that you are committed to serving the vision and mission of your church — both publicly and privately.

BE HELPFUL
Don't use your information about this ministry as ammunition against your pastor, but as encouragement for your pastor. Share good books, practical ways to engage and opportunities to connect with other pastors/leaders who have a shared heart for this.

BE PATIENT
Don't expect things to change overnight. Do what you can with what you have today then do what you can tomorrow with what you have tomorrow. In the end, these kids are worth the long, hard work it may require of you.

To dive deeper, watch this 9 minute talk on "How to Handle a Church Leader That Doesn't Get It". (Direct Link: **https://vimeo.com/126966037**)

DO YOU SUFFER FROM
THE CURSE OF KNOWLEDGE?

Sometimes we don't remember what it's like to not know something. For example, I would be an awful kindergarten teacher. Why? Because 1+1=2, and I'm not sure why that's so hard to understand?!

Of course I'm kidding, kind of, but that's a good example of the curse of knowledge — when we know something and forget what it's like to not know it. We have trouble putting ourselves in the other person's frame of mind. What seems so simple to us might not come across as that simple to someone else. We're all guilty of it at times, and we've all fallen victim to it as well, maybe when talking to a doctor, an engineer or any other expert in their field. They use words and illustrations that don't make sense to the layman. They suffer from the curse.

In a famous psychological experiment, a group of subjects was divided in two: tappers and listeners. The tappers were given a set of familiar songs (i.e. Happy Birthday, The Star Spangled Banner, Mary Had a Little Lamb, etc.) to listen to in headphones and told to rhythmically tap the songs on a table, while the listeners were asked to listen and figure out which songs the tappers were tapping.

The tappers were 50% certain that the listeners would be able to identify the songs they would be tapping, but the results of the experiment were shocking: only 2.5% of the songs were correctly identified by the listeners! In other words: the tappers way overestimated their tapping abilities!

The problem is that tappers have been given knowledge — they hear the song in their head. It's impossible for them to not hear it, and therefore incredibly difficult to put themselves in their listeners state of mind. There is a tune playing in their head that their listeners can't hear.

When we suffer from the curse of knowledge, we are like the tappers: we hear the foster care, adoption and orphan care song loud and clear in our heads. How can we not? Many of us eat, breathe and sleep with that song pulsating through every part of who we are and what it's made of our family. Why wouldn't others hear it the way we do? So we think maybe if we would just tap hard enough and loud enough, they will. Do you see where I'm going with this?

If you're not careful, the foster care, adoption and orphan care song that you sing can begin to sound like nothing more than an incessant tap in the ears of your pastor. This isn't to say you should stop singing the song. It just means that tapping louder and harder doesn't help. It really only hurts and the result is frustration — you won't understand why your leadership isn't "getting it" and they won't understand why you're won't stop tapping on them.

The only remedy to the curse of knowledge is to transform the way you communicate. Not by tapping louder and harder, but by putting yourself in your listener's state of mind and figuring out ways to help them begin to learn the song for themselves — word by word, note by note, line by line. So that eventually, by God's grace, they might start singing it for themselves one day.

As a father I'm constantly reminded that I have to contextually adapt my language on a regular basis. I have to speak to my 6 year old differently than I do my 8 year old, and both differently than I do my 10 year old and 12 year old. If I speak to my 6 year in the same terms I speak to my 12 year old in, she'll stare at me confused and eventually walk away. Of course I want my 6 year old's capacity for understanding and communication to grow and develop, but I have to learn how to communicate with her where she is now in order to help her grow into where she needs to be one day.

Take an honest evaluation of all the ways you potentially suffer from the "curse". Thank God for giving you this beautiful song to sing, and ask Him for the wisdom and patience required to help others start singing it to. Through your faithful perseverance they no doubt will!

2

GATHERING THE INTERESTED AND INVOLVED

PAVING THE PATHS

It's been suggested that when developers were building The University of California, Irvine campus, they constructed all the buildings but did not install sidewalks until the following year. They were testing the "path of least resistance", or "desired line" theory — the idea that people will naturally find the shortest, easiest and most desired path between point A and point B. We've all seen it — a trail cut in a field from where people have naturally created a walking path across it. That's the "desired line" — the path of least resistance to the other side of the field.

The following year, UCI identified where students had naturally cut paths between buildings and constructed sidewalks on top of them. In essence, they "paved the paths" — identifying where students were already walking and laying some solid foundation there.

Before you begin laying ministry foundation, perhaps the best thing you can do is identify where people in your church are already walking — then lay some foundation there. Community first, then ministry. Before we tell our people what we are going to do, let's first find out what they are already doing, then find ways to serve and support them in that. Ministry practices will naturally and inevitably flow from environments where the interested and already involved are connected in community and encouraged to walk together along the paths God has already laid out for them.

CREATING SMALLER CIRCLES

This simple graphic is a visual of what it could look like when you engage the crowd of your church (larger circle) and gather the interested and already involved into smaller circles of community together (smaller circle).

Whatever passion was once isolated within each one of them individually is now given the opportunity to collectively burn together — better, bigger and brighter. Ask God to continue to put kindling around it. See what happens.

SUGGESTIONS FOR HOW TO ENGAGE PEOPLE IN COMMUNITY:

• Invite them to a social event — a BBQ, family day at the park, etc.

• Host an informational luncheon after church. Share stories, cast vision and connect.

• Form a small group where you'll read a book or walk through a study together on the subject of God's heart for the orphan.

• Research local and national orphan care conferences, workshops or forums and take a group from the church with you.

• Simply meet one-on-one over coffee with people who share a similar heart as you.

These are just a few examples of the endless amounts of opportunities you have to begin connecting people into community around God's heart for the orphaned and vulnerable. Be creative!

PLANNING A "BRIDGE" EVENT

"Bridge" events are mid-size gatherings that create a pathway for people to move from the crowd into community. It's an important pathway to build, as many people might find that journey daunting. It can be intimidating to move from a place of anonymity in a church service, let's say, into a place of intimacy with people you don't know very well. That's a pretty big leap, and why bridge events are important.

As we've discussed, there's power in getting people that share a similar passion in the same room together. It takes individuals and turns them into community — a place where they can find support, encouragement and clarity along their journey. It also helps create critical mass for ministry growth. If you can get 10, 20, 50, 100 people in a room around a common cause it speaks volumes to those attending — "We're not in this alone!" — and to the leadership overseeing — "People are getting involved!"

HOW TO PROMOTE A BRIDGE EVENT

Generally speaking, you should allow approximately one month to promote your bridge event. The most ideal scenario is when the whole church is engaged with a sermon or announcement or promotional video, etc., and then the bridge event is the clear and simple follow up action item — "In response to today, sign up for this event."

It is important you not just announce the bridge event once, but that you continue to announce it every week leading up to the event in a variety of ways — i.e. stage announcement, postcards/flyer/bulletin, website announcement, emails, personal invites, etc. Every church chooses to promote key events in different ways. Find out how your church does it and take advantage of as many of them as you can every week leading up to the actual event.

The following chart is a sample of what your promotion strategy might look like:

ONE FULL MONTH OF PROMOTION

WEEK 1	WEEK 2	WEEK 3	WEEK 4	WEEK 5
FIRST ANNOUNCEMENT	SECOND ANNOUNCEMENT	THIRD ANNOUNCEMENT	FOURTH ANNOUNCEMENT	THE BIG DAY! FINAL ANNOUNCEMENT

MID-WEEK PROMOTION OPPORTUNITIES

CHURCH-WIDE EMAIL NEWSLETTERS

WEBSITE

SOCIAL MEDIA

ETC.

For many church leaders, announcements are the "Achilles heal" of their worship services — when's the best time to do them, how, and are people really listening? But perhaps they don't have to be so bad. With some simple changes and a little bit of strategy behind them, announcements can become one of the most impactful components of your worship gatherings. Be strategic in how you announce your bridge event. Consider "giving" people the following five things in order to broaden the effectiveness of your communication and maximize the impact of your event.

GIVE PEOPLE . . .

SOMETHING TO LOOK AT:
Some people learn audibly, many others learn visually. Consider the reality that in an average church service you have a variety of different types of learners that process and retain information differently. One person may simply need to hear the announcement; another may need to "see" it. This can be easily accomplished through a well-designed slide on the screen that is being projected while the announcement is being made. Very helpful.

SOMEWHERE TO GO:
It's as simple as, "We're hosting a luncheon, and if you have any questions we'll be at the info table in the hall after service." Or, "We're hosting a gathering and there's more information on the website." They've now heard an announcement about your bridge event, but they've also been told where they can go to learn more about it. Very helpful.

SOMETHING TO HOLD ONTO:
Don't just give people something to listen to, but give them something to hold onto that reminds them about what they've heard. It could be a blurb in the bulletin or a postcard in their seats. By giving them something tangible you've extended the life of your announcement — they heard it once that day, but now they'll be reminded throughout the week every time they see what you've given them. Very helpful.

SOMEONE TO TALK TO:
Announcements, events and scheduling can often sound very logistical and organizational; all the more reason to help make it personal and relational for your people. It can be as simple as, "We're hosting a luncheon, and if you have any questions you can talk to Sue Smith at the info table or email her at sue@suesmith.com." You've given them a real life human being to connect with. Very helpful.

SOMETHING TO SIGN UP WITH:
The point of all of this is to get people to attend your bridge event, which is why you should never announce any details of the event without having an opportunity for people to immediately sign up for it. It could be a portion of the bulletin, on the postcard you left in their seats, at an info table in the hall after service or an online form — or all of the above! By giving people some easy and immediate way(s) to sign up for the event you increase your chances of capturing them in the moment and the likelihood of them attending. Very helpful.

Throughout the 4–5 weeks you are announcing the event, continue to reinforce these five critical connection points. In other words, before you tell everyone in your church what the event is and how they can get involved make sure the appropriate mechanisms are in place for them to actually do that.

WHAT IF I DON'T HAVE THE STAGE?

Even if you are not able to have the event announced church-wide, it is still imperative to have a promotion plan in place, and to work the plan as diligently as you can. It will likely be more "grass roots", dependent upon personal invites, emails, social media posts, passing out postcards or other more unconventional methods of promotion.

Are there other places in the church you might gain access to in order to help get the word out? What about a note home with each child in the children's ministry? A small blurb in the weekly bulletin or church newsletter? A few posts on the church's main Facebook page?

Get creative. Identify a few key platforms you can utilize to help promote your bridge event, develop a plan and diligently stick to it. In the end, sometimes the more hidden, viral and word-mouth pieces of information become the most powerful forms of communication.

WHAT'S THE BEST BRIDGE EVENT TO PLAN?

While we've suggested a variety of different things you could do for your bridge event — an info meeting, a social gathering, a luncheon, etc. — we want to strongly suggest that while anything you do to connect people with each other will be beneficial, there's one that seems to be the most impactful: a lunch after your worship service.

Why is a luncheon so impactful? Here's a few reasons:

• Free food. No explanation needed!

• Once they leave it's much harder to get them back. Take advantage of the fact that people are already at church that morning. (This rule applies even for those churches that only have evening services — replace "lunch" with "dinner" or "coffee and desserts".)

• Child care can be offered. Whether you meet in your own building or use a rented facility, you most likely have classrooms for children set up on campus. Recruit volunteers (or pay professional childcare workers) to manage classrooms so parents can attend the luncheon and know their kids are being watched and fed.

• Sharing a meal is a natural form of fellowship. Rather than sitting people in rows of chairs for a "meeting" they can sit in circles together at tables to eat, connect and get to know one another.

It's for reasons such as these that we strongly suggest you host a luncheon (or some variation of that) for your bridge event. It helps to remove barriers to attendance (food provided for free, childcare provided for free, immediately following church) and creates a relaxed, welcoming environment for people to connect and be encouraged to take the next steps.

FOUR THINGS TO DO AT A BRIDGE EVENT

The goal of your bridge event is to help people feel connected, inspired and informed. On average you will have 60–90 minutes together in a luncheon setting. Of all the things you can do during that time, here's four strategic and essential things you MUST do:

SHARE STORIES

Set aside as much time as necessary to allow people to introduce themselves. They can answer a few simple questions for the rest of the room or small group at their tables: Who are you? Married? How long? Kids? How many? — Why are you at this luncheon today? What has your involvement in orphan care been?

INTRODUCE LEADERSHIP

Generally speaking, when people don't know where to go or who to talk to about something, they won't go anywhere or talk to anyone about it. It is important you use the bridge event as an opportunity to introduce your ministry leadership. It could be one point person or a full-blown ministry team. Either way, in introducing the leadership in front of the group you answer those two very important questions for people — where do I go and who do I talk to? Now they know.

CAST VISION
Vision is painting a picture for others of what the future looks like in a tangible and concrete way. It is important you answer three fundamental questions when sharing the vision of your orphan care ministry: 1) Why are we doing this? 2) How are we going to do it? 3) What are we going to do?

DEFINE NEXT STEPS
It's imperative to spend time during a bridge event letting people know what they can expect to happen after the bridge event is over. They should leave the room with a very clear understanding of what is coming next, when it's coming, where it's coming and why it's coming. When you increase clarity you reduce anxiety. The goal is for people to leave with a clear, actionable plan.

QUESTIONS TO CONSIDER WHEN GATHERING THE INTERESTED AND INVOLVED

❷ In what ways are you valuing the role of community in your ministry — not just in theory, but in practice? Name a few actual, current examples:

❷ In what ways is your ministry "paving the paths" — specifically responding to and meeting the needs of those on the foster care or adoption journey?

❷ What specific things would you like to see implemented in the next 3–6 months and 6–12 months to intentionally reinforce the value of community?

3–6 MONTHS

_____

_____

_____

6–12 MONTHS

_____

_____

_____

3
CLARIFYING VISION

As has already been stated, a visionary sees what does not yet exist, but communicates it as if it does. They not only believe certain things should happen, they also show people how they can happen. What do want to see happen? What steps do you need to take in order to make those things happen?

Your answers to these questions provide the framework for the vision of your ministry — a framework that is essential to construct as you build a leadership team and grow your ministry. If the vision isn't clear, then people won't know where you're headed — and if they don't know where you're headed, they'll start heading in their own directions. Clarifying vision, values and focus is essential to long-term effectiveness and sustainability of your mission.

INCREASE CLARITY, DECREASE ANXIETY

It seems no one gets lost anymore. When was the last time you stopped to ask for directions? With GPS tracking technology and little "Siri" voices in our phones, there's rarely a lack of clarity about how to get to where we need to go. Because technology has increased our clarity, our anxiety levels decrease — even when traveling to places we've never been before. Why? Because Siri will tell us how to get where we're going.

The vision of your ministry should increase clarity and decrease anxiety. It should communicate values, mission and direction in such a way that those involved in your ministry know where you're going, why you're going there and how you're going to get there.

Vision is not just seeing where you're going, it's also showing others how to get there.

———————

THE "SHOULD" VS. "CAN" PRINCIPLE

Part of clarifying your vision is understanding the difference between "should" and "can". Not every "can" is a "should", but every "should" must have a "can". Let's break that down.

Just because you "can" do something doesn't necessarily mean you "should". Can you run through the grocery store with a gorilla costume on screaming at the top of your lungs? Yes, you probably can. But should you? That's right, you probably shouldn't (please don't)! What you "can" do is not always what you "should" do, but what you "should" do must always have an actionable plan to actually do it — a "can".

Should you mow your yard so that it doesn't turn into the neighborhood jungle that attracts all the wild animals in the area? Yes, you probably should. Can you? Now, that's a great question that's a bit more complex. There's factors to consider — do you have the time, the right equipment, are you healthy enough to do it, etc.? Answering the "can" question is a bit more complex than the "should" question — it requires some creativity, planning and strategy in order to accomplish the task at hand. Should your yard be mowed? Yes. Can you? Well, yes, I have the right equipment, but there's more to consider. When I have time I'll do it on my own. However, if I don't have time that week, or I'm not feeling well, I have the number of a lawn service I can call to step in and take care of it. That's the plan.

MISSION CRITICAL MINISTRY

"Shoulds" are mission critical — if you don't do them you ultimately won't see the vision of your ministry materialize. They are, as the name suggests, critical to fulfilling what it is God is calling you to do. A clear vision creates parameters through which every opportunity can be filtered through the following questions:

Is this opportunity mission critical? Does it ultimately point us back to the vision of our ministry and help that vision become a reality? Or, does it distract us from it — or even worse, derail us from it?

If it's not mission critical, then whatever opportunity it is in front of you, although likely a "can", is definitely not a "should".

THREE PRINCIPLES TO CONSIDER

The more complex something becomes, the harder you have to work to create clarity within it. We all understand how to plug a lamp into a socket. From our perspective on one side of the wall, it's clear. Get behind the wall, however, and things become far more complex. Very few of us understand how electricity actually works.

As your ministry grows it will become more complex, and therefore that much more difficult — and important — to maintain clarity.
If you're in the early formations of your ministry, or are taking a step back from an existing ministry in order to redefine values and refocus efforts, here's three principles to consider as you set strategic priorities moving forward:

SIMPLE
The temptation is to say yes to every good "idea" and launch or lead the ministry with as much impact as possible. Yet, simplicity and focus are essential to effective, sustainable ministry. That requires being willing to say no at certain times, not yes all the time. Everything can't be a "should". It's more important to do the right things than it is to do many things.

SLOW
The goal of your ministry is sustainability, not speed. Moving too fast too soon can end up doing more harm to the ministry than help. The last thing you want to do is inadequately equip and prepare people only to have them burn out in the end. We have to develop realistic expectations for what we can accomplish effectively with what we currently have to work with.

SMALL
Starting small is not meant to imply that we don't want to set big goals for our ministry and believe God for big things. It's simply suggesting that in order to see both those things happen there may be some things we need to consider doing first. If we put the time in learning how to crawl, we'll eventually learn how to walk — and then run! But we have to start somewhere. Build a strong foundation first!

THE ART OF "SCALING" YOUR VISION

 To "scale" something simply means to take something big and complex — like the foster care crisis in your city or the global orphan crisis in our world — and make it more manageable for people to wrap their minds around. It is essential for your leadership team to "scale" the vision of your ministry in such a way that people in your church can see it, understand it, grasp on to it and engage with it. The goal is not to minimize the magnitude of the crisis at hand, but to provide a platform upon which your people can more easily see the problem and more readily identify their role in helping to solve it.

A "SCALED" STATEMENT
For example: "We want to eradicate the foster crisis" is not a vision. It sounds good and noble, but doesn't paint a clear picture for people. It's too big and heavy and lacks direction. The average person would buckle under the weight of a statement like that. It needs scaling. Perhaps something like this: "Our county needs 60 more foster families; we want at least 30 new families in our church to open their homes in the next year." That's clear and bold, but more manageable, actionable and achievable. People can wrap their minds around that vision.

MINISTRY ACTIVITIES
This includes casting vision for the different ministry activities you hope to accomplish over the next year, like "We want to open a foster family supply pantry, host an informational luncheon for people interested in getting involved and recognize Orphan Sunday".
Clear and achievable goals.

MAKE IT PERSONAL
It also applies to how you message your ministry to your people. While the needs are overwhelming, it's far more realistic — and more personally challenging — to focus on how each individual can change the world of at least one. Everyone can do something to change the world of at least one. That's the message. A clear vision much more difficult to discard.

If vision is painting a picture of the future then in these scaled statements, the future is clear.

QUESTIONS TO CONSIDER WHEN FORMING AND CLARIFYING YOUR VISION

❷ What is the vision of your ministry?
In one or two sentences, communicate the values, objectives and direction of your church's orphan care ministry.

❷ Where are you going in the next 6 months?
What are your most "mission critical" activities or objectives over the next 6 months?

❷ Why are you going there?
How do those mission critical activities point back to and reinforce the overall vision and values of the ministry?

❷ How are you going to get there?
What resources do you need in order to achieve those objectives over the next 6 months? Do you already have them? If not, how will you get them?

4

ARTICULATING A COMPELLING MESSAGE

In the flurry of all the things that come with leading and implementing ministries, one of the most critically important yet often overlooked components of ministry leadership is establishing clear and consistent messaging. What are we going to say? How are we going to say it? Why are we going to say it that way? How often will it be said? Who needs to be saying it?

These are crucial questions that must be rallied around as a ministry leader or leadership team. If we're not saying the right things in the right ways at the right times, our planning and events and calendars may be well organized, but our people will be far less likely to engage in them.

Among other things, the goal of your message is to:

• Provide clarity: A consistent message clearly articulates vision and direction. An inconsistent one is confusing, leaving people wondering what your ministry is doing, why it is doing it and how it is going to get it accomplished.

• Reinforce values: A consistent message repeatedly communicates what is most important to the ministry — in concept (what you believe) and practice (what and how you do it).

• Deconstruct false paradigms: A consistent message feeds your audience language and perspective that helps them formulate better understandings of the nuanced and complex issues your ministry is addressing.

• Articulate "why": People care more about why you do what you do than they do about what you do or how you do it. A clearly articulated "why" establishes trust, builds cohesiveness and motivates people towards the "what" and "how."

❷ What other benefits of establishing a consistent message can you identify?

❷ How have you experienced some of these benefits in your ministry?

❷ What changes do you need to make to ensure you are maximizing these benefits for your ministry?

THREE PILLARS OF A STRONG MESSAGE

1. A COMPELLING "WHY"

The first pillar of a strong message is a compelling why. The most inspiring messages motivate people with a sense of purpose bigger than themselves. They draw out and answer the question, "Why?" — Why is this important? Why are we doing this? Why should I care? Why should I sacrifice my time, money and energy to be a part of this? A truly compelling "why" casts vision, reinforces values, motivates people and gives them something bigger than themselves to believe in, pursue and sacrifice for.

As church leaders, it's easy to loose sense of our "why". Not because we fail to believe in something bigger than ourselves, but because we end up investing so much time and energy communicating what we're going to do and how we're going to do it that we're left with little time or emotional energy to cast vision for why we are doing it. We have a 5k race, a backpack drive, an informational meeting, a Christmas service project, etc. — here's what we are doing and how you can participate. But, why? What's the driving motivation behind it? What's the bigger purpose? What's the compelling reason for people to sacrifice their time, energy, money and family?

THE GOSPEL IS OUR "WHY"
We care for the orphaned and vulnerable because we have been greatly cared for in Jesus.

❝❞ *This is how we know what love is: Jesus Christ laid down his life for us. And we ought to lay down our lives for our brothers and sisters . . . let us not love with words or speech, but with actions and in truth.*
1 John 3:16,18

The work of Jesus on our behalf compels us to work on behalf of others. Why would we step into the hard? Why would we lean into the broken? Why would we open our families to the traumatic and difficult? Because that's what Jesus has done for us. We lay our lives down for others because He first perfectly, sacrificially and sufficiently laid down His life for us.

We care for the orphaned and vulnerable because we have been greatly cared for in Jesus.

———

He saw our brokenness and embraced us in our weakness, adopted us into His family and changed the course of our lives forever.

This beautiful picture of the gospel, and its vivid implications in our care of the orphaned and vulnerable, plays itself out through two primary aspects of theology:

   The Doctrine of our Adoption
   The Doctrine of His Incarnation

These two pillar doctrines form the strong and sturdy foundation of our "why."

The doctrine of our adoption
One of the most prominent pieces of imagery running throughout scripture, depicting the character of God and His work on our behalf, is the picture of family. Specifically, the illustration is rooted in the relationship between God as our Father and us as His dearly loved children.

❝❞ *See what great love the Father has lavished on us, that we should be called children of God! And that is what we are!*
John 1:12–13

The hinge upon which this entire new relationship with God has been formed is beautifully illustrated in scripture through the continuous use of the word "adoption". Passages such as:

❝❞ *He predestined us for adoption as sons through Jesus Christ.*
Ephesians 1:5

❝❞ *You did not receive the spirit of slavery to fall back into fear, but you have received the Spirit of adoption as sons, by whom we cry, "Abba! Father!"*
Romans 8:15

We were once outside the family of God but now, through the work of Christ on our behalf, have been adopted as dearly loved sons and daughters. We experience the rights and privileges of being known and loved as His! A new identity born out of a new way of how we relate to God — as our Father — and how He relates to us — as His children.

If our adoption into God's family is at the core of the gospel, then the gospel is certainly at the core of our calling to care for kids who need loving, safe and permanent families to call their own.

The theology of our adoption helps form the basis of our "why." Why would we care for orphaned and vulnerable children by bringing them into our families? Because that's what Christ has done for us.

But it doesn't end there.

Many leaders struggle to translate the doctrine of our adoption into the cultural fabric of their churches. The truth is we're not all called to adopt — or bring children into our homes through other avenues like foster care. So how does the doctrine of our adoption into the family of God practically translate into a message to our church that might not include adoption as an application?

Many church leaders stumble over the idea that, "We've been adopted into the family of God, but we're not all called to adopt". That's a hard message to communicate and an even more difficult and confusing one for people in our churches to hear. There has to be more, something broader and more holistic that has a variety of different applications for our people. A theological blanket, if you will, that can be laid out over the entirety of our church under which implications and applications for everyone can be identified.

This is where a distinct, yet intricately intertwined understanding of the doctrine of "incarnation" can be incredibly helpful to press into your messaging.

The doctrine of his incarnation
The word "incarnation" literally means to assume human form. The doctrine of Christ's incarnation speaks to God stepping into humanity, wrapping Himself in flesh and living completely and fully as both God and man. It's most notably recognized at Christmas with the birth of Jesus, yet its implications are far more pervasive than just on December 25th of every year.

❝❞ *All this took place to fulfill what the Lord had said through the prophet: "The virgin will conceive and give birth to a son, and they will call Him Immanuel" (which means "God with us").*
Matthew 1:22–23

The incarnation reveals much about who God is and what God does. It tells us He is the kind of God who sees broken and hard things and does not step away from them, but steps into them. He is "with us". He wrapped Himself up in our brokenness, carried our brokenness to the Cross, and was broken by our brokenness so that we don't have to be broken anymore. God saw us in our plight and moved towards us, not away. That's the gospel.

The Apostle Paul reiterates the incarnation of Christ and beautifully ties it into God's redemptive pursuit of humanity to make us His children, when he writes . . .

❝❞ *When the fullness of time had come, God sent forth his Son, born of a woman, born under the law, to redeem those who were under the law, so that we might receive adoption as sons.*
Galatians 4:4–5

Jesus was "born of a woman" (incarnation) in order "that we might receive adoption" (adoption) into His family.

The most inspiring messages spend less time telling us what to do and more time reminding us of who we are.

——

If the incarnation of Jesus is at the core of the gospel, then our stepping towards the hard and broken is certainly at the core of our calling to care for vulnerable kids. The theology of Christ's incarnation helps form the basis of our "why." Why would we immerse — or incarnate — ourselves into hard and broken places? Because that's what Christ has done for us.

The implications of the doctrine of incarnation are broad. The opportunities for each unique individual in your church to "incarnate" themselves into hard and broken places are endless and full of creativity.

This moves the conversation beyond just foster care, adoption or orphan care in some capacity — although these are clear and vivid outlets for your people to respond (perhaps that's why James 1:27 describes leaning into the lives of the vulnerable as one of the purest and most undeniable reflections of the gospel). Incarnation, however, speaks to a renewed posture and perspective towards the world around us in all matters of justice, mercy and sacrifice.

The world says we should avoid hard and broken things, insulate ourselves from them and isolate our families from them. The gospel, however, suggests an entirely different posture and perspective. It compels us to "incarnate" — to step towards and wrap ourselves up in them.

This could include a person in your church engaging their neighbor, opening their home to foster care, investing in renewal initiatives overseas, partnering with human trafficking rescue efforts in your city, feeding the homeless and the list could go on.

The opportunities to incarnate ourselves into hard and broken places are endless and full of diversity. The application of incarnation in foster care and adoption efforts is clear and undeniable. Why would we immerse — or incarnate — ourselves into hard and broken places? Because that's what Christ has done for us.

Consider how the doctrine of incarnation acts as a compelling grid and guide for all aspects of your church's mission, outreach, care, benevolence and evangelism? In the end, we move towards, not away.

THE BEGINNING, MIDDLE AND END
At the core of our motivation to care for the orphaned and vulnerable is the heart of God demonstrated through the gospel on our behalf. It's the gospel — the story of Christ stepping into our brokenness (incarnation) and drawing us into the security and assurance of His provision and protection (adoption) – which acts as the grid and guide to not only why we must care for the orphaned and vulnerable, but also how we must care.

THREE THINGS THE GOSPEL DOES

It Compels Us Into It
The work of Jesus on our behalf becomes the primary motivation as to why we would work on theirs — He interjected Himself into our story, so we too interject ourselves into theirs.

It Sustains Us in the Midst of It
When the work of orphan care gets especially difficult, and we're left asking "Why are we doing this?" the gospel reminds us that the work is worth it — it gives meaning to the struggle and context to the difficulty.

It is Put On Display Through It
" *Caring for the orphaned and vulnerable is one of the purest and most undefiled demonstrations of the gospel the world will ever see.* James 1:27

In the gospel God says, "I see you where you are and I'm coming after you." Foster care and adoption are beautiful echoes of that same declaration.

We cannot neglect the gospel as the source and sustenance of our ministry. It is the beginning of our motivation, the sustaining power in the middle and the beauty put on display in the end.

It is our most compelling "why."

2. IDENTITY DRIVEN
The second pillar of a strong message appeals to a person's personal sense of identity. The most impactful messages are those that move people — not simply in what they do, but in who they are. We're not simply trying to motivate our church to do the right kinds of things, but more importantly we're trying to equip them to be the right kind of church. The same is true for individuals — an identity driven message focuses less on what they should do and more on empowering them in who they are — trusting that a right sense of identity will ultimately translate into a right sense of doing.

The most inspiring messages spend less time telling us what to do and more time reminding us of who we are.

" *... we are God's handiwork, created in Christ Jesus to do good works ...* Ephesians 2:10

APPEALING TO IDENTITY
In their book, *Switch: How to Change When Change Is Hard,* Chip and Dan Heath use a late 1970's wildlife conservation program from the island of St. Lucia to illustrate the power to motivate action by tapping into people's personal sense of identity.

The scene was as follows: The St. Lucian parrot, native to the island (the bird does not live anywhere else in the world) was on the brink of extinction. Paul Butler, a London college student, had studied the bird and was tasked with running a campaign to save the parrot.

He proposed three strategies to the St. Lucian government: 1) Increase the penalties for capturing the parrot; 2) Establish a protected parrot sanctuary in the forest; and 3) Run "rain forest tours" to raise money to be invested into the environmental landscape of the island.

However, the government didn't really have the authority to set these into motion on their own. They required legislative action, and therefore the public's support.

That public support never came, at least not in the way Butler thought it would. He quickly found that the St. Lucian people were largely unaware

of the problem — they had no idea the bird was in danger of becoming extinct. They also didn't care. The existence, or lack thereof, of the parrot had no bearing on their lives. It did not make things better or worse for them financially, relationally or socially. Butler realized his campaign to garner public support would need to move in an entirely different direction.

So he launched a public awareness campaign, not to highlight the plight of the bird, but to promote a sense of identity among the St. Lucians — identity that would result in action.

He set out to convince the people that St. Lucians "were the kind of people who protected their own." He aimed to establish a sense of national pride and closely tie people's personal sense of identity to it. "We protect our own" was the mantra he set out to establish among the people.

He printed bumper stickers, buttons, t-shirts and flyers. He went to the newspaper and radio and local magazine offices to run promotional ads about the "pride" of being St. Lucian. He even convinced local ministers to cite verses about stewardship and "taking care of what God has entrusted to you" during sermons. Over time, public support grew for saving the parrot, and the government introduced Butler's recommendations, which overwhelmingly passed.

Why? Because he took the time to cultivate a proud sense of identity among the St. Lucian people — "We protect our own." He then introduced an opportunity for them to act upon that identity — one of their own, the parrot, was in trouble, and needed them to do something about it.

Eventually, not only was the St. Lucia Parrot saved, but Butler's campaign was replicated in other places all around the world. The Heath Brothers use this as an example of how to motivate people to action. When you build people up with a strong personal sense of identity — they develop the strength to act.

OUTCOMES VS. IDENTITY

Generally speaking, people make decisions through two primary lenses: Outcomes and Identity. The outcome-oriented lens filters decision making through an assessment of costs and benefits. The identity-oriented lens filters decision-making through a lens that is more intrinsically motivated by something deep within.

OUTCOMES	IDENTITY
Counts personal costs.	Counts costs to others.
Makes decisions that will maximize personal satisfaction.	Makes decisions that will maximize benefit to others.
Asks questions like... What will it require of me? How will it make me feel? What are the long-term effects?	**Asks questions like...** Who am I? What kind of situation is this? What does someone like me do?

It is estimated that the average person makes approximately 35,000 decisions every day. Some impulsively, like the decision to scratch an itch; some logically, like the decision to purchase the less expensive bottle of shampoo at the store. In all of our logical decisions we are filtering through an Outcomes vs. Identity paradigm.

Consider a teenager (most of us have them, have had them or eventually will), What if one day they find themselves faced with the decision to drink at a party or not. The outcomes questions they may ask are: "How will it make me feel?" Good (at least tonight). "Will people think I'm cool?" Maybe. "Is it worth getting caught?" I don't know.

The identity questions they may ask include (note — these are the ones we want them asking!): "Am I the kind of kid that drinks at parties?" No. "What kind of situation is this?" One where I'm being given the opportunity to do something that doesn't fit who I am. "If I don't drink, am I okay with not being accepted into the "cool" crowd?" Yes. "What does someone like me do in a situation like this?" I don't drink (Even better, I don't go to the party in the first place!).

Now that you're an adult, maybe it's the decision to accept a new, higher paying but more demanding job. Right now your job affords you the flexibility you need to spend the kind of time with your family you want. You're home for dinner, you're at every weekend sporting event for your kids and you even have extra time to take your wife out on special one-on-one dates periodically. This new job, however, pays more and advances your career to the next level but will not be as flexible.

The outcomes oriented questions you may ask are: "How will accepting this new job maximize my own satisfaction?" Well, it will pay more, give me more notoriety and authority within the industry and will finally land me that corner office I've always dreamed of.

The identity questions might be: "Who am I and what do I value most?" Well, I am a husband and father that values time with my family over notoriety and prestige at work. "What kind of situation is this?" The kind of situation where I would have to sacrifice time with my family for the sake of work. "What does someone like me do in a situation like this?" I don't accept the job, even if it means my co-workers think I'm crazy, my salary stays the same and I don't get the views from my office window I want.

You and I, along with the people in our churches, are making thousands of decisions a day — and if we're honest, our natural bent is to assess the outcomes — "How is it going to make me feel? What's it going to cost me? What decision do I need to make in order to maximize my own personal comfort?" — without considering the deeper questions of identity, value and what it means to lean into the hard and broken.

A generic appeal of "there's kids in foster care and you should do something about it" or "there's millions of orphans in the world and you should care for them" (obviously exaggerated and oversimplified statements for illustration purposes) falls on the ears of people that are assessing costs and maximizing comfort. They need a more compelling "why"! Why would they purposefully and intentionally step towards hard and broken things when everything inside of them is telling them to pursue comfort and convenience?

This is why it is vitally important for us to call them to a deeper more fuller way of thinking about their identity — and its implications — in light of the gospel. The goal of your message is to move people in your church from an outcome-oriented decision making paradigm to an identity-oriented one.

That's what Paul Butler did with the people of St. Lucia — he moved the islanders from outcomes-oriented thinking ("What difference does it make if we save the bird? It doesn't effect our lives that much.") to identity-oriented thinking ("We are St. Lucians, we protect our own — and one of our own is in trouble.")

It's important to note, cultivating an identity-oriented paradigm does not mean ignoring or negating the reality of outcomes. It's still vital to consider the costs, requirements and implications of certain decisions. However, identity reminds us that our decision making does not terminate on our outcome-oriented thinking. It assesses and validates the outcomes and then moves us into deeper, more intrinsic questions of values, worth and ultimate purpose.

"What's it going to cost me?"
 — A lot.
"How's it going to make me feel?"
 — Tired, sometimes empty and uncomfortable.
"What are the long-term effects?"
 — I don't know.
"But who am I?"
 — I am a broken person that God stepped towards, not away from,

and invited me into the security and provision of His family through the work of Jesus.

"What kind of situation is this?"

— A broken one where a child needs a family or someone just needs a hand.

"What does someone like me do in a situation like this?"

— I step towards it, not away from it — and accept the costs as worth it.

We consider the costs as worth it for the gain a child and family might receive. That's our compelling why!

In light of our compelling "why" (gospel), we want to be the kind of people (identity) who see hard and broken things and step towards them, not away from them. We count the costs (outcomes) of engaging in the lives of the vulnerable and orphaned as worth it — a natural outworking of the joyous privilege we have to put the gospel on display in pure and undefiled ways.

The goal of our message is simple: to move people from counting the costs to considering three very important questions:

"In light of the costs . . . "

1) Who am I?

2) What kind of situation is this?

3) What does someone like me do in a situation like this?

3. SPACE FOR EVERYONE

The third pillar of a strong message is one that empowers the whole, not just a few.

The most powerful messages tap into the collective diversity of the audience. They clearly establish there is space for all, not just a few. They provide rails upon which the wisdom, resources, perspectives, experiences and gifts of the whole can be utilized with greater force together than they ever could apart. The message for your church must be clear — everyone from the single, the married, the young, the old, the rich, the poor — each individual has a unique and vital role to fill.

THE BODY OF CHRIST

The imagery of a human body is consistently used throughout Scripture to illustrate the identity and activity of the Church — how the people of God relate to one another and function together. Some are hands and some are feet. Some are fingers and some are toes. Some eyes and some ears. We're a collective diversity of unique individuals coming together — all with different gifts, passions, resources, experiences and capacities — recognizing our differences and bringing them together for the common good. Scripture likens it to the way a physical body works — different parts, same purpose.

We're not all called to do the same thing, but we're all certainly capable of doing something.

❝❞ *For the body does not consist of one member but of many. If the foot should say, "Because I am not a hand, I do not belong to the body," that would not make it any less a part of the body. And if the ear should say, "Because I am not an eye, I do not belong to the body," that would not make it any less a part of the body. If the whole body were an eye, where would be the sense of hearing? If the whole body were an ear, where would be the sense of smell? But as it is, God arranged the members in the body, each one of them, as he chose. If all were a single member, where would the body be? As it is, there are many parts, yet one body.*
1 Corinthians 12:14-20

In the Body of Christ, no one is called to do everything, but everyone is created to do something. That's how our physical bodies work and that's how our churches work as well. Unique gifts are given to unique individuals, not for their own good but for the common good of the whole body.

❝❞ *For as in one body we have many members, and the members do not all have the same function, so we, though many, are one body in Christ, and individually members one of another.*
Romans 12:4-5

The proper functioning of the people of God to fulfill the purposes of God are most often portrayed in communal terms, not individualistic ones. While one role may be more visible and another more subtle, both operate on a cooperative level of equal codependence, to the extent that if even one seemingly "small" part suffers, like stubbing a toe, it effects the larger whole, like bringing a grown man to his knees in pain.

Likewise, when one part fulfills its role, like a hand holding a fork, the larger whole benefits, like a mouth chewing and a stomach being satisfied. This is what it means for the different parts of the body to be "members of one another." We are far more intricately linked than we realize.

Specifically, as we look at how the cooperative efforts of the Body of Christ work themselves out through the care of the orphaned and vulnerable, we find the same premise to hold true — we're not all called to do the same thing, but we're all certainly capable of doing something. We all have a role to play — some more visible, some more subtle — all of significant importance in serving vulnerable children and families well.

In the Body of Christ, there are no insignificant parts. The same is true for your ministry — everyone has a role to play, and they are all important

FIND YOUR SOMETHING

This becomes the consistent baseline narrative of your foster care and adoption ministry: Everyone can do something…FIND YOUR SOMETHING! This message continues to reinforce the identity-oriented decision making paradigm. The goal is not to fit a "square peg into a round hole," but instead to help people discover the unique gifts, talents, resources and passions God has given them and how they might be able to use those to serve kids and families. It helps answer the question, "What does someone like me do in a situation like this?"

A simple, consistent message at your church could be . . .

"At _____ Church,
some of us are going to bring children into our homes;
the rest of us are going to find ways to serve and support them."

AN "EVERYONE CAN DO SOMETHING" MODEL

This is just one example of what "everyone can do something" could look like. It can be one family bringing children into their homes while a whole team, in unique yet equally important ways, gathers around to serve and support them. Sometimes the best way to communicate your message is to show people what that looks like — visibly, tangibly and practically. Consider using an illustration like this:

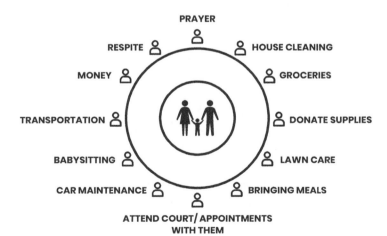

What would happen if everyone felt like they had to do the same thing? Or if no one ever told them of the different opportunities there were to get involved? This picture would look very different — incomplete and lacking all the necessary parts. Ensure your message is clearly and consistently communicating — both with words and visually — the "everyone can do something" model.

What could "everyone can do something" look like in your church?

SUPPORTING YOUR MESSAGE

As you establish your clear, consistent "everyone can do something" message, it is essential you build an infrastructure of opportunities to support that compelling call to action.

For example, if you tell people one way to support foster families is by becoming certified babysitters, it is important to educate them on the path they need to take in order to do that. Who do they talk to? When is the next class? What steps do they need to take? Can we do it at the church? Do we have to go somewhere else? Or, if people in your church want to help fund adoptions for families, ensure you have a clear path established for them to be able to do that. Does your church have an adoption fund? How do people designate their giving towards that?

The "rule" is simple — don't tell people there are a variety of ways to get involved without providing some clear, concrete and simple platforms for them to do it.

A three-tierd structure

It also is important that your "everyone can do something" message meets people where they are. Some are ready for higher levels of engagement while others need simple, "low-hanging-fruit" opportunities to get started. Consider structuring your levels of engagement into three primary categories, with a few opportunities to get involved under each.

Here are a few examples (lists are not exhaustive).

TIER 1 (Less commitment)	TIER 2 (Increased commitment)	TIER 3 (Highest commitment)
Bring meals Donate supplies Prayer	Babysit Financial Support Transportation/Errands	Foster Adopt Respite/Safe Families

Your "everyone can do something" message should include a variety of "on-ramps" for people to engage with a variety of commitments levels — that meet them where they are, empowering them to get involved and potentially move into deeper levels of engagement.

Full of creativity
The opportunities for the people in your church to get involved in caring for vulnerable kids, and supporting the families that do, are endless and full of creativity. Some ways are more "prescriptive" like babysitting, financially supporting, providing respite or donating supplies. Others might be more "descriptive" — unique and custom-tailored to the gifts, resources and opportunities of the individual. Either way, the opportunities to get involved are as unique and diverse as each individual member of your church.

Your clear and consistent "everyone can do something" message is designed to inspire your people to consider their role and empower them with the courage they need to take the next step.

I recently met a man in Kansas City. Mid to late 60's. He told me he makes the best BBQ in the state (a bold claim!) and LOVES to cater any foster care ministry related event at their church including respite nights for couples, info meetings for those considering getting involved and even taking meals over to families homes who have had a new child placed with them. Here's a guy who has said, "I know what I can't do, and I know what I can do; I'm going to do what I can do well." He told me that while he and his wife may not be in a position to bring a child into their home, they can certainly do their best to bless those who are. I couldn't agree more.

What kind of "Kansas City BBQ" stories do you have in your church? Perhaps it's . . .
 • A mechanic who gives foster families free oil changes.
 • A restaurant owner who gives foster and adoptive families free kids meals.
 • A landscape company owner who gives discounts to foster and adoptive families.
 • A beauty spa owner who gives foster and adoptive moms discounted services.
 • A college student who can't foster or adopt but can definitely babysit!
 • A web developer who builds platforms of communication for his church's ministry.

The list could go on. The opportunities are endless, full of creativity and as unique and diverse as each individual member of your church. The goal of your clear and consistent message is to inspire and empower them to "find their something."

Sharing a diversity of stories
It's important that your ministry is consistently sharing stories of how God is moving in the lives of families in your church. It's even more important that your use of stories is helping, and not unintentionally hurting, the broader vision of your ministry. When using stories — whether video, print or live interview style — ensure they are reinforcing the "everyone can do something" message. Otherwise, if it's only stories about families bringing children into their homes, the message being communicated is loud and clear...and confusing to those who likely won't ever do that.

Consider sharing stories of people who have never brought children into their homes but have still found unique ways to be involved. Share stories of those who have financially supported adoptions, have wrapped around foster families, have come alongside families in crisis to help prevent foster care from becoming a part of their story, or even of those who have not yet done anything but are in the process of prayerfully considering how God is calling them to get involved. What has God taught them in those spaces? How have they been impacted as a result?

The reality is that the majority of people in your church will likely never bring a child into their home, but will in the end be the bearers of some of the most powerful stories of what God is doing through your ministry and in your church.

Where are your "BBQ guy" stories and how are you sharing and celebrating them?

APATHY, OR LACK OF CLARITY?

It seems no one gets lost anymore. When was the last time you stopped to ask for directions? With GPS tracking technology and little "Siri" voices in our phones, there's rarely a lack of clarity about how to get to where we need to go. With the increase of clarity brought about through technology, our levels of uncertainty have decreased — even when traveling to places we've never been before. Why? Because Siri will tell us how to get where we're going.

In their book, *Switch*, Chip and Dan Heath speak to the issue of clarity when they say, "What looks like resistance is often just a lack of clarity." In other words, it might appear like someone doesn't care, but what if they actually do care and just don't know how to care? That's a big difference.

The point, as we've previously discussed, is when we increase clarity for people we help decrease things like uncertainty, anxiety and apathy in them. When they know how to get where they want to go it helps build confidence for them to act. The "everyone can do something" message brings the clarity many need to engage in something they've always cared about but were never just quite sure how to care about it!

This changes everything about the assumptions we make and the strategy we take. Rather than assuming people don't care and placing the burden on them to start caring, perhaps it's appropriate at times to assume people do care and place on the burden on us, as leaders, to show them how to care! Maybe what looks like resistance in your people is actually just a lack of clarity in them. Your "everyone can do something" message, and the stories you celebrate to reinforce the message, can empower your people with the clarity they need to get involved.

What aspects of your ministry's message are not increasing clarity and decreasing uncertainty for people? What changes can you make to help bring more clarity to what an "everyone can do something" ministry looks like?

CONCLUSION

We're not all called to do the same thing, but we are all capable of doing something.

This is your constant, consistent, compelling message and is reinforced every time anything is ever publicly said or written about the vision of your foster care and adoption ministry. Everyone. Can. Do. Something. Singles, college students, newly married, young families, empty nesters and retirees. Everyone.

Let's recap a few helpful things to consider as you continue to build out your "everyone can do something" culture:

l Theologically outline the design and function of the Body of Christ.

l Visually communicate a strategy that everyone can plug into.

l Build "tiers" of engagement for people to meet them where they are.

l Share stories that reflect the creativity and diversity of opportunities.

l Flip assumptions and pursue clarity in your ministry's messaging.

The goal of your message is simple: to empower people to use the unique gifts, passions and resources God has given them for the good of the whole. Each individual member doing its part so the whole body can function better together for vulnerable kids and families.

That's the goal.

BUILDING A COMMUNICATIONS "DRIP STRATEGY"

Develop a strategy for how you are going to consistently communicate God's heart for the orphaned and vulnerable, and provide opportunities for your people to get involved throughout the year.

Big events like Orphan Sunday or a sermon are like "fire hydrants" — a lot of information and emotion all at once for our people to swallow. These "fire hydrant" events are powerful, acting as significant catalyzers to movement by sharing a strong vision with a wide audience.

However, it would be counterproductive to host one or two special "fire hydrant" events during the year with little to no mention of adoption, foster care and orphan care in between. That rhythm does not provide opportunities for people to process what they've heard, what they're feeling and what perhaps their next steps are. It leaves them overwhelmed with a lot of information and nowhere to take it.

It also subtly communicates a message we don't intend to communicate — that is, that our church cares about this ministry . . . a couple of times per year. Of course we know that is not the case — we care about this all the time — but to our people, if we're only addressing it once or twice a year, we could perhaps unintentionally communicate something contrary.

In between the periodic floods, we also want to consistently "drip" the care of the orphaned and vulnerable on our people throughout the year in smaller, easier to absorb ways.

This gives them the opportunity to process through what they are hearing and feeling, and discern how God may perhaps be calling them to respond. It also keeps the message in front of our church on a more consistent basis.

To accomplish this, consider outlining a "drip strategy" for the year (or maybe just start with 6 months) that helps keep the message in front of your people in a consistent way — with both large "fire hydrant" events and more subtle "drip" opportunities.

SAMPLE ONE YEAR DRIP STRATEGY

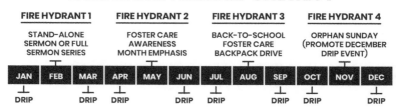

EXAMPLES OF HOW TO "DRIP"
Sermon illustrations, Stories (live, video, print), Foster/adopt parent social gatherings, Informational meetings, Introductory classes/small groups, Parent dedications, Service projects, Etc.

These are simply example "fire hydrant" and "drip" opportunities your church could take part in. Be creative, use the familiar and identify things in your church that are "normal" that could be utilized in annual communications, event and programming plans like this. Find things that fit the culture and rhythm of your church.

It's likely that your church is already doing some things that could be included, so beware of "reinventing the wheel" or duplicating efforts.

The ultimate goal is for the care of the orphaned and vulnerable to be consistently incorporated into the overall messaging of the church.

MAKING ORPHAN CARE "NORMAL"

In a counterintuitive way, the goal of your church is not to make caring for the orphaned and vulnerable a "special thing"; it's to make it a "normal" thing. It's relatively easy to make foster care or adoption a special thing because in many ways it is special. It's a uniquely difficult yet rewarding place to engage a broken world with the heart of God.

Yet for as special as it is, we don't want it to be a "special" part of our church that we only talk about at "special" times of the year and only "special" people are involved in. Instead, we want it to be a "normal" thing at our church that is "normal" to hear about all the time and "normal" people are involved with it.

Articulating a consistent message, both in content — "everyone can do something" — and in frequency — developing a "drip strategy" — will help to normalize the ministry in your church. When asked, "Who can be involved with this ministry?" the aim is that your people say, "Anybody can!" When asked, "Is it normal to hear about foster care and adoption at your church?" the hope is for your people to unhesitatingly answer, "Yes!"

The goal is not to make caring for the orphaned and vulnerable a "special" things; it's to make it a normal thing, and oddly enough that a harder hill to climb. But it's not impossible. Be creative, strategic and realistic as you consider how to incorporate it into the normal fabric of your church.

5

ENGAGING THE WHOLE OF YOUR CHURCH

Central to effectively sharing your clear and consistent "everyone can do something" message is the development of a core strategy for how you will bring that message to bear to the whole of your church. What pathways will you build to carry your message to every member of your audience in a way they can hear, understand and respond to? How will you engage not just the few, but the whole of your church with God's heart for the vulnerable and orphaned?

In this section we will explore three key ingredients to effectively engage, empower and mobilize every person in your church — from the student to the single to the married, the young to the old, those with kids and those without — everyone.

THREE INGREDIENTS OF EFFECTIVE ENGAGEMENT

SHRINK THE PROBLEM
Shrinking the problem means presenting it in way that people can relate and respond to. It is not minimizing the problem, but communicating it in such a way so that solutions feel more manageable for your people.

GROW YOUR PEOPLE
Growing your people is discipleship — equipping and empowering them in both their awareness of their new identity in the gospel and the unique ways God has wired, resourced and gifted them.

CHART A PATH
Charting the path means establishing clear, fluid action items moving forward. It is the "next steps" tangible pathway for people to take that makes it easier for them to do the right things next.

There is no perfect "script" or "formula" for ministry, but there are principles that can be carried into any church context. The challenge for leaders is to contextualize these principles to the unique culture and rhythms of their own church community.

1. SHRINK THE PROBLEM

Suppose you asked me to help you lose 15 pounds. The problem is, you have a disease — a disease called "fast food"! You're addicted to the #1 value meal at your favorite restaurant which includes a burger, fries and a drink. You're eating it almost daily for lunch. We quickly identify this to be part of your problem.

What if I inform you that your favorite meal deal is a total of 1,100 calories. Sounds like a lot of calories, right? Yes, it is! But probably not enough to cause you to think twice about ordering that meal again. It tastes too good not to. Ask any fast food restaurant company and they'll say the same thing — people discard facts about their health for the sake of their own personal satisfaction. It's just what we do.

THE ART OF "SCALING"

But what if I were to scale it down for you into different terms and tell you that 1,100 calories is equivalent to eating nearly FOUR candy bars for lunch? Would you eat FOUR candy bars for lunch? Probably not. Yet, on a calorie level, that's essentially what you're doing with the fast food meal. A large number, like 1,100 calories, is intangible. We have no human experience tied to it, no frame of reference to measure its proportions by and nothing to compare it to. Also, has anyone ever really seen a calorie? Held one? Touched one? Not that I know of. They're these little, evil invisible things we know are out there but have no personal, tangible, relatable experience with.

Since we can't see them or feel them or comprehend the enormity of 1,100 calories, we discard the facts and choose taste over health. Four candy bars, however, is easy to see. It's more relatable to our human experience and much simpler to hold on to — literally. You can hold them, touch them, feel them and understand them, and therefore have a much more difficult time discarding the facts about them.

This is "scaling" — contextualizing something of grand proportions into more tangible, relatable terms. We've previously discussed this principle but it bears repeating in this context. In this case, from 1,100 to four. Scaling provides a smaller perspective through which we're able to better see, understand and grasp the bigger picture. It doesn't negate the reality or significance of the problem, it simply provides a platform upon which to engage with it more efficiently.

"SCALING" THE VISION OF YOUR MINISTRY

The statistics are daunting: millions of children around the world, hundreds of thousands within the United States, dozens of thousands within your state and city, hundreds and thousands within your community alone — all needing safe, loving permanent families. The problem is big, but with numbers like that it's hard for people to wrap their minds around what to do, where to go and how to even begin to be a solution to the problem. It's too hard to grasp and therefore too easy to dismiss. And most people do — they dismiss the facts for the sake of their own personal satisfaction, comfort and convenience.

Part of engaging the whole of your church includes scaling the crisis for them — in such a way that they can see it, understand it, grasp on to it and engage it more effectively. The goal is not to minimize the magnitude of the problem, but to provide a platform upon which your people can more easily see the problem and more readily identify their role in helping to solve it.

A "scaled" statement

For example: "We want to eradicate the foster crisis in our city" is not a vision. It sounds good and noble, but doesn't paint a clear picture for people. It's too big and heavy and lacks direction. The average person buckles under the weight of a statement like that. It needs scaling. Perhaps something like this: "Our county needs 60 more foster families; we want 30 of them to come from our church in the next year." Or, "There are 14 children in our county waiting to be adopted; we want our church to bring this number to zero this year." These are clear and bold, but more manageable, actionable and achievable. People can wrap their minds around them.

Make it personal

It also applies to how you challenge your people personally. Raising awareness about the 143 million orphans in the world, or the 450,000 kids in the foster care system is important, but easy for your people to discard with no real personal application that is "scaled" for them. Perhaps it is far more realistic — and more personally challenging — not to focus on changing the world for every orphan, but to focus on how each individual can change the world of at least one. Everyone can do something to change the world of at least one. A clear vision is much more difficult to discard.

QUESTIONS TO CONSIDER

❶ In what ways is your current message helping to "shrink the problem" for your people by giving them clear, tangible, relatable pieces of information to act on?

❷ In what ways is your current message actually working in a counterproductive way — overwhelming and perhaps paralyzing people from acting?

❸ What specific things about your message can you change to help make it more relatable and actionable for your people?

❹ What pieces of information do you need to gather (i.e. smaller statistics locally or globally, specific needs that can be met in the community, etc.) that can be incorporated into your message?

2. GROW YOUR PEOPLE

❝❞ *Jesus came to them and said, "All authority in heaven and on earth has been given to Me. Therefore go and make disciples of all nations, baptizing them in the name of the Father, and of the Son, and of the Holy Spirit, and teaching them to obey all that I have commanded you.*
Matthew 28:19-20

We are not simply recruiting people to meet a need; we are discipling them to obey a command.

Many years ago while working with junior high and high school students, a mentor of mine was talking to our staff about the vision of our ministry. In reference to the students in our city, he said, "What we bring them in with will likely be what we keep them with." We wanted our ministry to students to be rooted in strong biblical teaching, authentic relationships and living on mission together — not entertainment. Of course we were going to have fun together, but the primary thing we held out in front of students each week was not how entertaining our ministry was to them, but how meaningful and valuable it was for them.

If we were bringing them in with entertainment, then what happens when they're no longer entertained by us, or something else down the road becomes more entertaining than we are? Our ability to entertain may have had the ability to bring them in, but it wouldn't have the power to keep them there.

However, if strong biblical teaching and deep rich relationships are what originally connected them to the ministry, then even when life is hard or not very entertaining — no matter the circumstances these students were going through — the truth of God's Word and loving, meaningful relationships would keep them connected. That's where we poured most of our efforts. That's what we wanted to keep them with.

WHAT ARE YOU BRINGING THEM IN WITH?

In a counterintuitive way, the goal of our ministry is not to recruit more families faster; it's to disciple the right families longer. That's how we "grow the people" — through discipleship. Not bringing them in with the "need," but growing them in the gospel and empowering them to act upon the need in front of them. While the need is overwhelming, it is ultimately the gospel that compels and sustains.

Obviously God is not opposed to us meeting needs. Over and over in scripture He reiterates the importance of meeting the needs of those around us:

❝❞ *What good is it, my brothers, if someone claims to have faith, but has no deeds? Can such faith save him? Suppose a brother or sister is without clothes and daily food. If one of you tells him, "Go in peace; stay warm and well fed," but does not provide for his physical needs, what good is that?*
James 2:14-16

We are not simply recruiting people to meet a need; we are discipling them to obey a command.

❝❞ *If anyone has material possessions and sees a brother or sister in need but has no pity on them, how can the love of God be in that person?*
1 John 3:17

Scripture is clear: Disciples — those who claim "to have faith" and to have "the love of God" in them — meet needs. That's just what disciples do. It is possible to motivate people to meet others' needs without becoming disciples of Jesus. However, it is impossible to be a disciple of Jesus and not meet needs. It's just what disciples do.

NEEDS-BASED VS. GOSPEL-DRIVEN
If we are primarily bringing people in with the need, we will need to keep them with that need. However, the problem occurs when the need gets too hard, too costly and begins to require too much. As is often the case, people are emotionally compelled in the moment to meet immediate needs, which is not always a bad thing, but can sometimes result in people not being prepared to stay engaged in the long and necessary work required to fully meet the need.

When their need to help has been satisfied or the need itself has become too much, they are likely to move on and leave the need for someone else to meet.

However, if we are primarily bringing people in through the gospel — growing them down deep in discipleship and empowering them to live through an identity-informed paradigm — our goal will be to keep them with the gospel. Even when the need gets hard or heavy or costly, the gospel gives meaning to the struggle and purpose to the process. It reminds people that their work is worth it. It keeps them.

The sustaining, refreshing power of the gospel has greater capacity to "keep" people engaged in the need. So we bring them in with the gospel, and we keep it in front of them always. The gospel is both a) what we bring our people in with (front-end motivation), and b) what we keep them with (back-end support).

FRONT-END MOTIVATION } (👪) { **BACK-END SUPPORT**

FRONT-END MOTIVATION
The gospel compels us to speak on behalf of and stand for the sake of those who cannot speak and stand for themselves — because that is exactly what God has done for us through Jesus. It is our "why."

We do not motivate our people into this with the hope of the gospel and then leave them hopeless when the journey gets hard. Instead, we remind them that the same gospel which compelled them will also provide the hope they need to sustain them.

BACK-END SUPPORT

Foster and adoptive parents need support, but the kind of support they need is varied and will come through a dynamic set of mediums — all of which are critical, but none of which is ultimately sufficient on its own.

FOUR ESSENTIAL AVENUES OF SUPPORT

1. TANGIBLE

Families who are opening their homes to foster care and/or adoption may need a variety of different practical items — such as meals delivered, baby supplies, furniture, help with transportation, etc. While this list is certainly not exhaustive, here's eight simple, unique and diverse ways that your church can tangibly serve foster and adoptive families:

Organize a Meal Calendar
It's fairly standard practice for small groups, support groups, women's ministries, etc. to organize a meal calendar for a family when a new baby is born. Do the same for a foster family when a new child is brought to their home.

Schedule Lawn Care
Do whatever you can to relieve any amount of burden you can from the family — like organize a team of people in the church who rotate mowing foster families lawns while they have children in their homes.

Certify Babysitters
It is illegal to leave a foster child with a babysitter that is not (in most cases) CPR certified and background checked. This means most families struggle to find babysitters. Host CPR certification classes at the church. Have sitters ready for families!

Conduct Dedication Ceremonies
Most churches celebrate Parent/Child Dedication ceremonies during the year. Do the same for foster families. When they bring in a new placement pray for them in front of the church and have the body commit to support them!

Host Date Night Childcare
Once a quarter or every semester (or even once a month) the church can hire certified babysitters for a Friday or Saturday night and allow foster families from the church and community (hint: outreach!) the chance to go on a date!

Deliver Care Packages
Most placements occur with little to no notice. Often times within hours. Have things like diapers, gift cards, baby supplies, and other necessities ready to go to be dropped off to a family immediately after receiving a child.

Stock A Supply Pantry
In conjunction with the care packages develop a supply pantry that stores items like diapers, cribs, strollers, car seats, baby equipment, bikes and other things that families may immediately need upon a child placement.

Build A Respite Care Team

Certified babysitters can watch a child for a short period of time (generally less than 48 hours). When extended breaks are needed or travel plans require it, respite care providers are needed. These are extremely hard to find. Have a team at your church ready!

2. RELATIONAL

Foster and adoptive parents face a unique set of circumstances and experience a range of emotions that few outside of the foster care and adoption community can relate to. Give them a place to connect, share experiences and encourage one another. Remind them they are "not alone"in this journey that can sometimes feel very lonely and isolating.

3. EDUCATIONAL

As well, find ways to provide on-going training for parents who are opening their homes to children from hard places. Whether it's a monthly trauma-informed care training class, a series of videos, books, webinars or even attending conferences on the subject, be consistent about putting helpful information in front of your families who are loving children that have been riddled by the effects of trauma in their lives.

4. SPIRITUAL

The gospel sustains your people in the process of caring for kids and families and refreshes their souls when weary. It provides perspective through the difficulties and struggles and reminds them of their "why" throughout. As you are able to help them connect regularly, continue to provide the prayer and spiritual support they need to continue on this journey in a healthy, gospel-centered and sustainable way.

Consider how the back-end support your church is providing foster and adoptive families can in some capacity incorporate all four of these elements — tangible, relational, educational and spiritual — into one cohesive system. Perhaps it is a monthly gathering, support groups, private Facebook groups, email newsletters, regular "nights out" for moms, dads, couples, periodic trainings, etc. Again, get creative and be consistent.

It might also mean working in collaboration with other churches, agencies or organizations in your area. If your church has a few families you might not be ready to offer a whole host of comprehensive support, but perhaps partnering with another church that has a few more families and another church that has a few more would lead to a strong, more robust collaborative effort to support all of your families together better than you could have apart.

Back-end support is crucial. When families feel supported by their church and their community of people around them, their capacity to endure and thrive through the fostering or adopting process exponentially increases.

3. CHART THE PATH

As we have already discussed, increasing clarity decreases anxiety — not just in how you communicate your vision, but also in the actionable "next steps" you provide for your people.

Where is your ministry going? How are you getting there? What are the steps people need to take?

Who should they talk if they have any questions? Where should they go if they want more information?

These questions, and many others just like them, are "path" related questions. They're directional and tangible — they tell people where to go and give them the resources they need to get there.

Leadership isn't just telling people where to go, it's giving them what they need to succeed along the way.

Are the answers to your "path" questions clear for your people? If not, a clearly defined "path" will become essential in helping your people know where the ministry is heading and how to get involved.

IDENTIFYING YOUR PATH

Right now your ministry is likely operating in one of two different environments:

"Top-Down"

The leadership of the church is driving the vision and implementation of the ministry, either exclusively or in close partnership with lay/volunteer leaders. Church resources like stage time and finances are utilized for promotion, awareness and engagement.

"Bottom-Up"

The leadership of the church is either not "on board" with the ministry, or supports it in principle but not in practice. Little, if any, church resources are allocated to support the ministry. It's largely driven in a grassroots way through passionate advocates.

The first step to charting a clear path is identifying where your starting point is: Are you currently working in a "top-down" culture or a "bottom-up" culture?

A "TOP-DOWN" PATH

A clear "top-down" path starts big and moves people into smaller levels of community and discipleship where they can find connection, support and clarity as they identify their role and take their next steps.

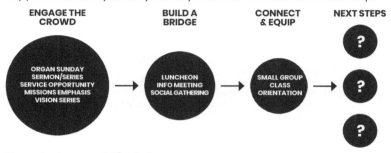

ENGAGE THE CROWD — ORGAN SUNDAY SERMON/SERIES SERVICE OPPORTUNITY MISSIONS EMPHASIS VISION SERIES

BUILD A BRIDGE — LUNCHEON INFO MEETING SOCIAL GATHERING

CONNECT & EQUIP — SMALL GROUP CLASS ORIENTATION

NEXT STEPS — ?

Your strategy could include:

• Recognizing Orphan Sunday, or preaching a sermon on God's heart for the vulnerable and orphaned. (engage the crowd)

• Hosting a follow-up luncheon or informational meeting where people can connect, hear vision and learn more. (build a bridge)

• Facilitating a class or small group study building a theological framework, establishing realistic expectations and identifying next steps. (connect & equip)

• Connecting people to their "next steps". Examples include a local foster care agency, adoption agency, support team coordinator, etc. (take next steps)

Key Principles:

Do not implement one stage without having the next step planned (example: Engage the Crowd on Orphan Sunday AND be ready to announce the "Bridge" event — perhaps an informational luncheon — immediately).

This four-stage rhythm can become a consistent engagement process in the church, perhaps starting once a year, then twice a year, then once a quarter.

Just like with pre-marital counseling, we walk couples through a process before the wedding day. Similarly, before connecting families with outside agencies, consider the importance of journeying with them through this connection and equipping process.

In it you can help them more deeply understand God's heart for this, more confidently identify their role in this, more realistically set expectations for what it is going to be like and more effectively surround them with the resources and help they will need to thrive. That's what we do for engaged couples before making a lifelong covenant with one another on their wedding day. Why not do the same for families preparing to potentially make a lifelong covenant to a child, and the process required to care for that child?

A "BOTTOM-UP" PATH

A clear "bottom-up" path starts with the foundation of community. It works to build community among those already involved before starting a ministry to engage more. The goal is to identify what culture already exists in your church, who is already involved and how can the ministry be built to best serve and support them. Then it expands from there.

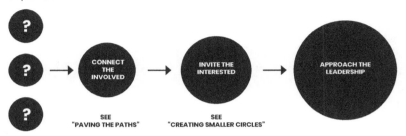

Your strategy could include:

Identify who in the church is or has been involved with foster care and adoption in some capacity and invite them to a social gathering. (connect the involved)

Over time, begin expanding the circle by inviting those who have expressed interest in getting involved. (invite the interested)

Eventually, begin approaching the leadership of the church with a proven model and a realistic, strategic plan moving forward. (approach the leadership)

Key Principles:

Ask, "When was the last time we had everyone in our church who is fostering/adopting or has fostered/adopted in the room together?" If never, start there.

The legitimacy of your ministry is not compromised by the fact it's not driven from the top; it simply means the trajectory of your ministry will look different.

Nearly everyone involved has had someone express interest to them in some way. Examples: "I've always wanted to do that" or "My husband and I have been praying about that." Invite them into the next phase of your community.

Approach your church leadership with strong proof of concept for the ministry (built upon the community you have formed). Demonstrate the work you've already done, not all the work you're asking them to do.

6

BUILDING A DISCIPLESHIP PIPELINE

Discipleship is not an event, it's a process. It's the long, sometimes slow and sometimes tumultuous journey of movement — from where we are to where we need or want or hope to be. Discipleship toward a goal or vision doesn't just happen — it requires intentionality, purpose and planning.

Often times when we think of the ministry of Jesus we're quick to recall some of the more obvious things He did — He preached, He healed, He performed miracles — and we tend to overlook one of the most fundamental, yet subtle things — He discipled. He journeyed along with 12 men for years, teaching them, loving them, equipping them and even watching them take one step forward and two steps back at times. At the core of Jesus' ministry was discipleship — the process of moving fishermen to become "fishers of men". (Matthew 4:19)

As we have previously discussed, the goal of your ministry is not simply to recruit more people to meet a need, it's to disciple more people to obey a command. But how do we do that? What elements of movement are crucial to establishing an effective and sustainable process for moving our people towards caring for the vulnerable and orphaned or supporting those who do?

In this section we will explore five elements of sustainable movement you can utilize and contextualize as a grid of discipleship in your own church.

They include . . .

FIVE ELEMENTS OF SUSTAINABLE MOVEMENT

1. USE THE EXISTING
The answers to what you need are often found in the things you already have.

2. SET MICRO GOALS
Set goals small enough to reach yet still meaningful enough to strive for.

3. CONDUCT SMALL EXPERIMENTS
Sometimes the greater goal of something isn't success, but learning.

4. INSPECT WHAT YOU EXPECT
Establishing accountability measures for goals and action items.

5. CELEBRATE SUCCESSES
Create a culture that recognizes, reinforces and rewards the "wins."

ELEMENT #1 USE THE EXISTING

Main Idea:
Use what you have.

Jesus spoke all these things to the crowd in parables; he did not say **" "** *anything to them without using a parable.*
Matthew 13:34

THE MINISTRY OF JESUS

The brilliance of Jesus' teaching style was found not just in the message He delivered but also in the way He delivered the message. He used what He had, often using parables — simple stories that conveyed profound messages — to illustrate things He knew His audience would be able to relate to. Pictures like a woman baking bread (Luke 13:20), a mustard seed (Matthew 13:31-32), references to sheep and goats (Matthew 25:31-41), and so on. Jesus used "the existing" around Him as the pipeline through which He would change people's lives.

He did this in other ways as well — spitting in the dirt to create mud that would restore the sight of a blind man (John 9:1-12), breaking a loaf of bread to illustrate His impending sacrifice on the Cross (Matthew 26:26), instructing fishermen to cast their nets to put His power on display (John 21:6). These were things already existing and available for Him to use in His ministry.

What resources, ministry structures, programs and tools does your church already have that can be utilized in this ministry? Instead of creating something new, in what ways can you "use the existing?"

RIGHTING FAULTY ASSUMPTIONS

It's often assumed that in order to launch new ministries in a church, new programs need to be started, new leaders need to be trained and new resources need to be gathered. In order to make the ministry "big" we need to do "big" things. Yet to an already busy ministry calendar and spread thin leadership team, the idea of starting a lot of "new" can sound overwhelming and simply impossible.

While in some circumstances it might be necessary to introduce many "new" things into a church's system in order to launch a ministry, in other cases churches might find that a new ministry focus can be introduced through "existing" mechanisms that are already in place.

Think of it this way . . .

FALSE	TRUE
Your church will need to add many new programs to do this ministry well.	Your church already has many components it needs to do this ministry well.

DEVELOPING INTEGRATED CULTURE

The following two charts of examples are certainly not exhaustive, but merely descriptive of the types of departments, ministries or focuses that might already exist in your church. Use these charts as launching pads for creativity. What "existing" areas inside your church and outside your church could you potentially utilize for your foster care, adoption and orphan care ministry?

UTILIZING THE EXISTING INSIDE YOUR CHURCH

This diagram suggests some examples of ministry activity INSIDE your church that can occur in partnership with your orphaned and vulnerable ministry. They are a snapshot of the types of opportunities your church has to more strategically and intentionally establish an integrated approach to child and family welfare using other existing church ministry programs and resources.

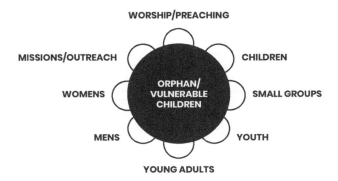

What if the conduit God is going to use to embed His heart for the vulnerable into your church is not the pulpit, but the existing platform of your children's ministry? Maybe it will be happen through opportunities and resources disseminated through kids into their parents' hands and their families as a whole. Or maybe your existing small groups ministry will act as the primary vehicle not only for front-end discipleship but also back-end support? Think about the opportunities that already exist in your church. Perhaps it will be a bit more "unconventional" than you initially thought, but in the end better for the ministry and your church as a whole?

UTILIZING THE EXISTING OUTSIDE YOUR CHURCH

This diagram suggests some examples of ministry activity OUTSIDE your church that can occur in partnership with your orphaned and vulnerable ministry. They are a snapshot of the types of outreach and mission ministries your church is likely already involved with that have a direct correlation back to the issues of foster care, adoption and orphan care.

What specific existing programs or structures inside and outside your church can you utilize to more effectively build an integrated OVC ministry?

DEVELOPING A HOLISTIC MINISTRY CULTURE

BREAKING DOWN SILOS

Churches tend to default into a "silo" of ministries — "That's the missions ministry over there," "That's the homeless ministry over there," "That's the orphan care ministry over there," etc. In reality, however, many of these justice, mercy and hospitality-oriented ministries are not mutually exclusive. They are on some level interconnected — all part of the same child and family welfare continuum intersecting at different points along the way.

For example, a church could be deeply involved in rescuing and bringing restoration to victims of the growing human trafficking industry. This is a critical place for the Church to engage, however many do so without the knowledge that a significant percentage of those trafficked are actually alumni of the United States foster care system. With that added piece of knowledge, now, a church could more holistically engage the fullness of the problem — to not only bring restoration to those victimized through various programs, but also to prevent more from becoming victims by providing loving homes for children in the foster care system in their city.

Now, it's no longer the foster care ministry "over here" and the human trafficking ministry "over there." The silos begin to break down and a more holistic approach begins to emerge — one which addresses the problem in a fuller way by both restoring those victimized by it and preventing others from becoming a part of it.

Similarly, a church could be deeply involved in issues of homelessness, racial reconciliation, mentorship, prison ministry, global child sponsorship programs, and so on — all of which, and others, fall along the same continuum of caring for vulnerable and orphaned children. As well, some internal ministries within the church — things like children's ministry, singles ministry, youth ministry, young adult ministry, benevolence ministries, counseling ministries, etc. — can all be storehouses for a foster care, adoption and orphan care ministry. It no longer has to be the student ministry "over here" and the foster care ministry "over there," but instead can be a more intertwined and dynamic network of ministries.

THE RIVER
Imagine three friends come upon a raging river. They see children in the water rushing down the rapids towards a waterfall. One friend immediately jumps into the river and begins pulling as many children out as he can. Knowing there's a waterfall downstream, the second friend runs down river and tries to catch as many children as he can before they fall over the cliff. The third friend, however, wonders why these children are in the river in the first place. He runs upstream to find out how he can put a stop to it. All three friends are running in three different directions, each addressing different yet equally important points of the problem — there are kids in the water and we need to get them out.

FRIEND 3   FRIEND 1   FRIEND 2

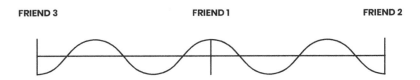

THE CHURCH

The responses of these three friends is a powerful image with parallels to orphan and vulnerable children ministry that are helpful as we consider and seek to establish a holistic, comprehensive and strategic ministry approach in our churches.

MID-STREAM INTERVENTION

Generally speaking, orphan care in the Church has been deduced to foster care and adoption — to jumping into the raging child welfare river mid-stream and pulling as many kids out as fast as we can. This is a right and necessary place for the Church to be. There are literally thousands of kids in our country and millions worldwide needing someone to intervene on their behalf. If not us, then who? But that's not the totality of what the Church can or should be doing. This perspective is too narrow and siloed. It fails to consider how these kids found themselves in this position in the first place (up-stream), and what the trajectory of their lives statistically looks like (down-stream) if no one intervenes on their behalf now.

DOWN-STREAM RESTORATION

It's typical for churches to be involved in various types of down-stream justice and mercy efforts — whether feeding the homeless, ministering to the incarcerated or engaging in ministries committed to rescuing victims of sex trafficking, etc. However, they're often doing so without a clear understanding of how interconnected the plight of those cross sections of people are to the larger continuum of child welfare. A significant percentage of incarcerated males, the homeless community and girls who are trafficked into the sex industry (down-stream) have at one point in their lives spent time in the child welfare system (mid-stream). When viewed through a more holistic and comprehensive lens, we'll find that if we really want to effectively engage some of these "down-stream" ministries we must also look back up-stream and consider how those in need of restoration found themselves in these positions to begin with.

UP-STREAM PREVENTION

As well, when we consider how these kids end up in the river in the first place, we realize that before we have a foster care crisis in our country we have a families-in-crisis crisis in our country, and before we have an orphan care crisis in our world we have a families-in-crisis crisis in our world. Orphan care is not just about caring for orphans, it's also about caring for families in crisis up-stream in order to prevent their children from ever finding themselves in the river mid-stream. The questions should both haunt us and drive us — Where are these kids coming from, and how can we prevent them from ending up in these awful places? Consider how your church can run upstream to do whatever is necessary to prevent kids from ending up in the river. This is a right and necessary — and albeit messy and difficult — place for the Church to be.

Not only is it essential for your church to establish an "everyone can do something" holistic message, it's equally important to begin taking steps towards developing a holistic approach to how you are engaging in the child and family welfare continuum — from Prevention to Intervention to Restoration — in a balanced and sustainable way. A strategic approach to the continuum reinforces and supports the "everyone can do something" message — everyone can jump into the river somewhere, somehow.

The chart below suggests some examples of ministry activity that can occur at each stage along the continuum. By no means are these lists exhaustive, nor do they address the fact that some ministries can span the entirety of the spectrum in and of themselves. However, they are a snapshot of the types of opportunities your church has to more strategically and intentionally establish a holistic approach to child and family welfare at every point along the same continuum.

PREVENTION	INTERVENTION	RESTORATION
Child Sponsorship Programs	Foster Care	Prison Ministries
Pregnancy Assistance	Adoption	Homeless Ministries
Centers	Orphan Care Support	Sex-Trafficking Recovery
Safe Families	Recovery Programs	Transitional Living Programs
Mentor Programs	Mentor Programs	Education Services
Family Development Programs		

INTERCONNECTED CULTURE NOT ISOLATED MINISTRIES

DIFFERENT OUTWORKINGS OF THE SAME MINISTRY ALONG THE SAME CONTINUUM

The objective now is to lay all your ministry activities out on the table and identify where, if and how they fall along the "river" of child and family welfare. If you're not able to easily identify where something fits then perhaps it's time to make the hard yet worthwhile call to get rid of it. Find where you're strong, be honest about where you're weak, and be brave enough to make the necessary decisions in order to more effectively and strategically engage child and family welfare in a broader, more holistic way — from prevention to intervention to restoration.

QUESTIONS TO CONSIDER

❷ How does developing a holistic and integrated approached to your orphaned and vulnerable children ministry open up more opportunities for the various types of people in your church to engage in a variety of ways?

❷ How does it reinforce your "everyone can do something" message?

❷ How does it aid in the discipleship process of your people?

ELEMENT #2 SET MICRO GOALS

Main Idea: Dream big, move small.

"" *It is better to take many steps in the right direction than to make a great leap forward only to stumble backward.*
Chinese Proverb

VIRTUALLY IMPOSSIBLE TO MISS

I do not enjoy running — at all — but I sometimes force myself to go and knock out a few miles in my neighborhood. While I'm typically dreading the process on the front end, by the time I make it back I'm always glad I did it — and even a bit proud!

In order to make the run more manageable and less dreadful, I've learned to set "micro-goals" along the way. Micro-goals are so small that they're virtually impossible to miss. My micro-goals are the light poles that intermittently line the main road from the front to the back of my neighborhood. I've found that if I focus on the larger goal only, let's say the 3-mile marker, it's much more difficult for me to mentally stay focused. I'm consumed by the "gap" between where I am and where I ultimately want to be. That "gap" is filled with distance, time and a lot of hard work. But, if I set smaller micro-goals along the way — simply focusing on making it to the next light pole 100 yards ahead — effectively shorten the "gap." This helps pass the time, establishes momentum and builds confidence along the way.

Ministry is a marathon, not a sprint.

And while we are all visionaries and see where we ultimately want to be, it's necessary — if not critical — to set micro-goals along the way. Otherwise, we'll burn out in the big gap, become disillusioned with the process and perhaps, worst of all, lose the joy we once had for the purpose that compelled us in the first place.

MARKS OF AN ACHIEVABLE GOAL

What types of goals should you be setting, and what particular aspects of your goals will help make them more likely to be achieved?

Let's use the acronym "S.M.A.R.T."

SPECIFIC | Where is the next light pole? What does it look like?

MEASURABLE | How do we know when we've arrived at the next light pole?

ACHIEVABLE | Do we believe it is possible to make it to the next light pole? Based on what? Past experience of making it to other similar light poles? A sheer determination of will and core conviction that we have to make it there?

REALISTIC | What conditions would need to exist in order to make it to the next light pole? Do those conditions exist now? If not, can we create them?

TIMELY | What specific amount of time are we giving ourselves to make it to the next light pole?

Setting "SMART" goals means knowing where the "finish line" is and identifying the "street lights" along the way that will help you get there. It's setting a strong, yet healthy pace for the ministry providing the necessary support, encouragement and motivation people need to endure through the "gaps" and persevere in joy.

What next steps can you take that are so simple they'll be virtually impossible to miss? Maybe it's an event at your church, recognizing Orphan Sunday this year for the first time, recruiting a few families to bring meals to a new foster home? Perhaps it's getting 5, 10 or 20 families to attend an informational meeting about foster care and adoption? Or maybe it's simply inviting those in your church who are fostering or adopting over to your home for a BBQ to begin building community among them.

SETTING YOUR MICRO GOALS

Consider having your ministry team participate in this simple two-part exercise:

1. Identify your long-term vision. What does the finish line of the marathon look like for your ministry?

2. Map out your 6-month, 12-month and 24-month micro-goals. Where are the light poles along the way?

LONG-TERM VISION

_____

_____

_____

MICRO-GOALS

6 MONTHS

_____

_____

_____

12 MONTHS

_____

_____

_____

24 MONTHS

_____

_____

_____

Where are your light poles? Make them so simple you can't miss them, and then later on we will discuss the importance of celebrating those small victories along the way!

Ministry is a marathon, not a sprint.

——————

ELEMENT #3
CONDUCT SMALL EXPERIMENTS

Main Idea:
Take risks, fail and learn.

"" *I didn't fail 1,000 times; the lightbulb was an invention with 1,000 steps.*
Thomas Edison

LEARNING TO FAIL

Thomas Edison is one of history's greatest inventors, despite making 1,000 unsuccessful attempts at inventing the light bulb. When asked, "How did it feel to fail 1,000 times?" Edison replied, "I didn't fail 1,000 times. The light bulb was an invention with 1,000 steps." Thomas Edison's willingness to try, fail and learn changed the world forever.

Michael Jordan is heralded as one of the greatest basketball players of all time. When asked about his success, he replied, "I've missed more than 9,000 shots in my career; I've lost almost 300 games; 26 times I've been trusted to take the game winning shot...and missed. I've failed over and over again in my life. That is why I succeed." Michael Jordan's willingness to try, fail and learn changed the game of basketball forever.

Steve Jobs was fired from Apple in 1985. Several years later he retook the helm, and in a Stanford commencement speech said this of his being fired: "I didn't see it then, but it turned out that getting fired from Apple was the best thing that could have ever happened to me . . . It freed me to enter one of the most creative periods of my life." Steve Jobs' willingness to try, fail and learn changed the face of consumer technology forever.

BE WILLING TO "EXPERIMENT"

A soccer-themed poster hangs in my oldest daughter's room that reads: "You miss 100% of the shots you don't take." The message? Don't be so afraid to miss that you never actually shoot.

The same is true in your ministry — don't be so afraid of a new thing not working that you don't ever try anything new. What if the goal is not merely success (although of course we want new ministry ideas and efforts to "work")? What if it's more than that? What if it doesn't "work" the way you hoped it would, but you still learn something valuable from the experience that you can now carry with you in ministry? Perhaps that — being willing to learn and grow — turns what might feel like failures into invaluable successes.

WHAT IS A "SMALL" EXPERIMENT?

A small experiment is one that, a) helps grow the ministry if it "works," and b) does not compromise the ministry if it doesn't "work".

Let's present a case study about a new ministry's experiment in one church that didn't "work":

The "Small" Experiment: Hosting a foster care informational meeting.

Outcome: Low attendance.

Impact on overall ministry: Minimal. No major positive or negative outcomes.

Lessons learned: They discovered, 1) promotion was weak (few people knew about it) and, 2) the meeting time was inconvenient (7:00pm on a weeknight).

Action items: Develop a one-month promotion campaign and schedule the meeting for a Sunday right after service. Provide food and childcare for free.

Outcome of 2nd event: Higher attendance; momentum produced for the ministry.

Instead of the ministry leaders feeling like "it didn't work because no one in our church cares about foster care," they instead decided to learn from the experience and implement some new strategy moving forward.

The goal of a "small" experiment is to learn. Among other things, trying things and failing can teach you more about:

- the people you are serving
- the culture of your church
- the environment in which you are doing ministry
- the leadership temperaments of your ministry team
- the effectiveness (or lack thereof) of your communications/promotions
- the clarity of your vision
- the clarity of your message
- etc.

FAITHFULNESS OVER OUTCOMES

Ministry Leader: God is more pleased by your willingness to be faithful than He is concerned about your ability to achieve a certain outcome through it. "Well done, good and *successful* servant?" No. "Well done, good and FAITHFUL servant." Faithfulness is our success, not achieving some outcomes that only God has the capacity to produce.

Of course we want to see measures of health and growth and impact achieved in the ministries we lead, but what happens if it never gets as big as we want, we don't have as many families fostering or adopting as we hoped for, or if our pastor or church leaders never fully get on board? What happens if our definition of "success" in ministry never materializes? Does this mean we have failed? Does this mean our work was in vain? Is it really worth it in the end?

" " *We look not to the things that are seen but to the things that are unseen. For the things that are seen are transient, but the things that are unseen are eternal.*
2 Corinthians 4:18

You may not see it now — you may not ever see it fully in this lifetime — but what you are doing is of eternal significance. Fix your eyes there — on eternity — but be faithful here, today, and then tomorrow, and then next week, continuing to make those sometimes unseen deposits into peoples' lives, trusting God with the outcome as you experience the beauty and struggle of walking with Him along the journey.

READ HEBREWS 11:1–39

" " *29 By faith the people passed through the Red Sea as on dry land; but when the Egyptians tried to do so, they were drowned. 30 By faith the walls of Jericho fell, after the army had marched around them for seven days . . . 32 And what more shall I say? I do not have time to tell about Gideon, Barak, Samson and Jephthah, about David and Samuel and the prophets, 33 who through faith conquered kingdoms, administered justice, and gained what was promised; who shut the mouths of lions, 34 quenched the fury of the flames, and escaped the edge of the sword; whose weakness was turned to strength; and who became powerful in battle and routed foreign armies.*

" " *35...There were others who were tortured, refusing to be released so that they might gain an even better resurrection. 36 Some faced jeers and flogging, and even chains and imprisonment. 37 They were put to death by stoning; they were sawed in two; they were killed by the sword. They went about in sheepskins and goatskins, destitute, persecuted and mistreated — 38 the world was not worthy of them. They wandered in deserts and mountains, living in caves and in holes in the ground.*

" " *39 These were all commended for their faith . . .*

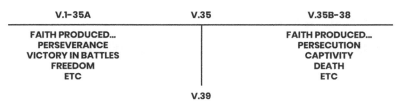

V.1-35A	V.35	V.35B-38
FAITH PRODUCED... PERSEVERANCE VICTORY IN BATTLES FREEDOM ETC		FAITH PRODUCED... PERSECUTION CAPTIVITY DEATH ETC

V.39

"THESE WERE ALL COMMENDED FOR THEIR FAITH..."

Notice the shift that takes place in v.35. We see how faith can produce significantly different outcomes. Some experienced great victories while others walked through horrific tragedies. In it all, God was pleased by their faithfulness and less concerned about the outcomes their faith produced.

QUESTIONS TO CONSIDER

❷ Have you tried something in your ministry that didn't "work" the way you hoped it would? How did that initially make you feel? What did you learn about your leadership and the ministry from the experience?

❷ What is one thing you have been considering doing in the ministry but for one reason or another have been afraid to try? How can you use it as a "small" experiment for your ministry?

❷ What hope do you find as a ministry leader in the fact that "God is more pleased by your willingness to be faithful than He is concerned about your ability to achieve a certain outcome through it"? How does this truth directly apply to your current ministry leadership role?

ELEMENT #4
INSPECT WHAT YOU EXPECT

Main Idea:
If you don't address it, you endorse it.

" " *Plans fail for lack of counsel, but with many advisers they succeed.*
Proverbs 15:22

MORE THAN JUST ACCOUNTABILITY

If you're a parent you have likely walked through a version of this scenario: You tell your son to clean his room. Some time later you walk in and find that the room appears to be clean. Upon further inspection you discover the room was not cleaned at all. Everything that was on the floor had just been relocated — shoved under the bed or hidden in the corner of the closet.
You say, "I told you to clean your room." He says, "I did." You then find yourself actually having to define what you meant by "clean your room" — for likely the dozenth time!

This is a classic case of "inspecting what you expect." You expected a clean room, so you inspected to determine whether or not the task had been completed — but not just completed — completed correctly. This is not an uncommon process in all of life — we're held to certain sets of expectations and structures put in place to determine whether they are producing the intended outcomes.

It's more than just accountability — did you complete the task? It's stewardship — are we leading this ministry and utilizing its resources in the most efficient and effective ways possible?

MEASURING OUTCOMES

Every ministry wants to be as effective as it possibly can be. Outcome measurement will help you understand whether yours is. With the information you collect, you can determine which activities to continue and build upon and which you may need to change in order to improve your strategy's effectiveness. There are several compelling reasons to measure outcomes:

To determine the effectiveness of a resource, program or event.

How do you know if a program within your ministry is effective? If it's not effective, would you want to know so it can be improved? How do you know if people are engaging with a resource, such as a Bible study or curriculum, you've chosen to utilize in your ministry? If they don't like it, would you want to know so you can find something different? How do you know if the people who attended an event you hosted found it to be a valuable use of their time? If they didn't, would you want to know so you can improve it next time?

To identify the most effective practices.
With the information and feedback you collect, you can determine which activities, resources or programs to continue and build upon, which to continue but modify, and which to stop doing altogether.

To reinforce clarity and consensus around the vision of your ministry.
Everyone in your ministry from staff to leaders to volunteers, should understand what is going on in the ministry and what it is ultimately intended to achieve. Inspecting what you expect by measuring outcomes, analyzing the results and identifying best practices moving forward helps to clarify vision, next steps and goals for the team.

THE "SO WHAT" TEST

Outcomes ask and answer the question, "So what?" So what if you had 20 families attend a foster parent support group. Did they leave more encouraged and connected than when they first arrived?

So what if you had 30 people attend a trauma informed parenting training. Did they walk away with the resources needed to help them parent better? And are they actually parenting better because of it?

So what if your team works with five local organizations in a collaborative alliance. Do those partnerships actually follow through in their efforts to get more and better work done together than they could separately?

The "so what" test is not meant to be an indictment, but actually an encouragement. It's a litmus test that can applied over all facets of the ministry to help you determine whether the time, energy and resources you are pouring in are producing the results you want.

IF YOU DON'T ADDRESS IT, YOU ENDORSE IT

It's like setting out to mow the lawn on a hot summer day and getting to the end, only to discover the engine was running but the blade was not spinning. How disheartening would that be!? All that work put in only to realize it wasn't doing what you thought it was. That's what the "so what" test does — it recognizes that if you don't address the problem, you ultimately endorse the practices that produced it. "So what if you're working hard to push that mower in 100 degree temperatures. Let's make sure the blade is spinning so the grass will actually get cut." The goal is to ensure your ministry is endorsing the most effective practices with the best possible outcomes.

OUTCOMES ORIENTED QUESTIONS
The main questions addressed in outcome measurements are:

What has changed in the lives of individuals, families, children and the community as a result of our ministry?
How has this program, event or resource made a difference?
How are the lives of those who participate in our ministry better as a result of our work?

Outcomes are not simply measured "numerically" — i.e. How many people attended the event? — but are ultimately determined "transformationally" — How is this event, resource or program changing the lives of people in our ministry?

FEEDBACK AND SURVEYS
Below are example feedback and survey form statements and questions. What others can you think of that would be helpful to use for your ministry?

STATEMENTS
(1–5 scale from "1 — strongly disagree" to "5 — strongly agree")

I came away better equipped for adoption, foster, and/or global orphan ministry because of this event, program, resource . . .

I would recommend this event/resource/program to a friend.

I am going to incorporate what I've learned from this material into my life.

QUESTIONS
What content or ideas would you like to see included next time?
Are you likely to attend this event again in the future?
Would you recommend this Bible study, curriculum or resource to a friend?
What was the most impactful thing for you about this event, program or resource?

SIGNIFICANCE OVER SIZE
Measuring outcomes through these lenses reminds your team of this simple truth: The success of your ministry is not determined by its size, but by its significance in the lives of those you are serving. It's about stewarding those God has entrusted to you in the most effective ways possible — whether it's 200 people, 20 or 2.

And again, at the end of the day faithfulness is our success, but we certainly want to do the best we can with what God has entrusted to us in the meantime.

QUESTIONS TO CONSIDER

❷ Here are some questions and concepts for your leadership team to consider as you assess the need for measuring the outcomes and effectiveness of your ministry:

❷ What outcome measuring mechanisms do you have in place for your ministry? Surveys? Feedback forms?

❷ If none, what next steps can you take to begin implementing opportunities for people to provide feedback in order to learn and improve for next time?

Most time and energy is focused on planning and execution of events and programs. How can your leadership establish the third critical component — back end assessment — into everything it does? How will that information be reviewed among the team to help build consensus and commitment to a unified vision moving forward?

ELEMENT #5
CELEBRATE SUCCESSES

Main Idea: Reward the "wins".

❝❞ *Plans fail for lack of counsel, but with many advisers they succeed.*
Proverbs 15:22

THE SIMPLICITY OF A GIFT CARD

The healthiest organization I've been a part of was led by a president who consistently rewarded "the wins".

During every weekly staff meeting the leadership would recognize the team member who experienced the greatest "win" that week and reward them with a $5 gift card to a coffee shop. A simple gesture that had a profound impact on the culture of our team, and ultimately on our organization.

Not only was the staff member being recognized by the leadership, they were being honored in front of the whole team and rewarded with something of value — a simple gift card. While the gift card may only be worth $5, the whole experience was invaluable for the team member who was the honored recipient of that week's award.
It continually reinforced a culture of celebration on our team and connected us with a shared sense of passion. While we wanted to experience the "wins" personally, we also wanted to see our teammates honored for their "wins" — which was often more fun to experience on their behalf than it even was for ourselves.

WHY CELEBRATE SUCCESSES

Here are five core reasons to establish a rhythm of celebrating the small wins of your ministry as you journey towards the long goal:

BUILDS MOMENTUM

It's exciting for people to see progress and energizing for them to be part of.

INCREASES COMMITMENT

Highlighting the positive outcomes of your ministry strengthens peoples' resolve to want to be active participants in what's going on.

FACILITATES COMMUNITY

Consistently celebrating others' "wins" unifies those involved in the ministry and tightens the bonds of connection and togetherness.

ESTABLISHES CULTURE

A culture that celebrates, honors and rewards is attractive and inspiring to be a part of.

REINFORCES VISION

When you celebrate the small wins along the way it provides opportunity to point to the bigger vision you are all journeying towards together.

PRODUCES HOPE

As we have discussed, ministry is a marathon, not a sprint. Every time another "light post" benchmark is reached, it produces hope that we can all actually make it to the finish line together.

"POSTCARD" CELEBRATIONS

The vision of your ministry is a "big picture". It's like a mural on the wall your church looks at and longs for. It's a beautiful, diverse, nuanced masterpiece of all kinds of people participating in caring for orphaned and vulnerable children in all kinds of ways. It's the "finish line" of your marathon, but along the way there are many "light pole" opportunities to stop and celebrate.

If your vision is the big "mural," then the small celebrations along the way are like "postcards" — smaller, easier to hold onto moments that remind your people of two things: 1) There is a mural we're all working towards, and 2) God's goodness and faithfulness to us are evident in each snapshot taken along our journey towards it.

"Postcard Celebrations" are smaller, easy opportunities to recognize what God is doing in peoples' lives through the ministry.

If your ministry is the large funnel, it begins with a variety of people engaging with it through different touch points. Some might be interested in foster care, others in adoption, still others might want to learn how to wrap around birth families or support other foster families in the church. There are an endless amount of reasons why people would initially engage, but the vision of the ministry catalyzes them together, in their diversity, along a unified path towards a big picture "mural" vision.

"Postcard Celebrations" can come in a multitude of forms: A family takes a new foster or adoptive placement, an informational meeting is well attended with many eager and excited people ready to get involved, more than enough backpacks were donated for the back to school drive that benefits a local foster agency, another child was adopted into a family in the church, etc.

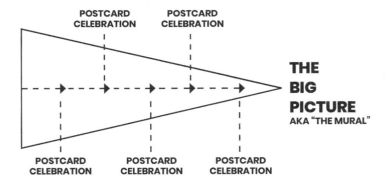

Be on the lookout, and have others on the lookout with you, for opportunities to put smaller "postcards" in peoples' hands that remind them of what the mural looks like and encourages them that God is guiding along the way, so there's much reason to celebrate!

ADDENDUM

GLOBAL ENGAGEMENT AND THE CHURCH
FREE RESOURCE

Impacting the world in significant, meaningful, Christ-honoring ways has always been a hallmark of the Christian church. Through local, domestic and global initiatives, God's people have historically led the way in compassionate awareness, advocacy and participation in matters of justice and mercy, renewal and restoration, hope and healing. Participation in ministry to orphaned and vulnerable children (OVC) and short-term missions (STM) has grown significantly in recent years.

This trend warrants much celebration, as the Church is increasingly engaging in matters near to God's heart. Yet, it also demands much caution. Although good intentions underlie this movement, we must be aware of the common principles and pitfalls in order to effectively and sustainably form strategic partnerships, engage cross-culturally, and send volunteers to support and serve vulnerable children, families and communities around the world.

The purpose of the *Global Engagement and the Church* eBook is to provide helpful information and tools for churches desiring to build an effective, sustainable and impactful global engagement strategy. It aims to provide a high-level introduction and overview of some key principles, practices and questions that are important to consider when developing global engagement strategies.

It is constructed around three primary elements:

1. Forming Healthy Strategic Partnerships,
2. Prioritizing Child, Family and Community Well-being, and
3. Participating in Short-term Missions Effectively and Ethically.

It then points to further resourcing that can be utilized to engage deeper in the most relevant or pressing topics for your team. Although every context is different, the ideas, principles and questions addressed in this resource will help build a framework as you seek to optimize your global engagement strategy.

To learn more, and to download your free copy of *Global Engagement and The Church*, visit **cafo.org/church**.

ABOUT THE CHRISTIAN ALLIANCE FOR ORPHANS

Christian Alliance for Orphans (CAFO) unites a global network of respected organizations and a national network of churches. Our joint initiatives inspire and equip Christians to live out effectively the Bible's call to care for orphans and vulnerable children.

CAFO Membership is an opportunity to join in a vision for God's glory and the care of orphans that is larger than any one organization or project. Together, we seek to inspire, interlink and equip God's people to reflect His heart for the orphan. To a watching world, the Alliance is an all-too-rare picture of the church unified, serving the fatherless in both word and deed, bearing poignant testimony to the character of our God.

THE NATIONAL CHURCH MINISTRY INITIATIVE

Through the National Church Ministry Initiative, CAFO helps churches build effective and sustainable ministries with essential knowledge, best-practice models, practical resources, strategic coaching and networking opportunities.

Visit **cafo.org** to gain access to:
- Custom one-on-one ministry coaching
- Free church ministry webinars and slide decks
- Regular newsletters filled with networking and equipping opportunities
- CAFO National Church Network membership information

WANT TO HOST A WORKSHOP?

If you want to bring the content of this book into a live workshop experience for your leadership team or a network of churches you are involved with, contact us at info@cafo.org to begin the discussion. We frequently travel to spend time with various groups and are capable of hosting different style sessions, from two-hour sessions to eight-hour trainings to full two-day workshops.

NOTES

NOTES

NOTES

NOTES

NOTES

NOTES

NOTES

NOTES

NOTES

NOTES

NOTES

NOTES

NOTES

CPSIA information can be obtained
at www.ICGtesting.com
Printed in the USA
LVHW082020161119
637582LV00004B/88/P